A GUIDE
— *for the* —
Scrupulous

SPIRITUAL PRACTICES
CRITICAL BELIEFS
HELPFUL PRAYERS

Rev. Thomas M. Santa, CSsR

Catholic. Pastoral. Trusted.

Imprimi Potest: Kevin Zubel, CSsR, Provincial
Denver Province, the Redemptorists

Published by Liguori Publications, Liguori, Missouri 63057

Liguori Publications, a nonprofit corporation, is an apostolate of the Redemptorists (Redemptorists.com).

Phone: 800-325-9521 Web: Liguori.org

A Guide for the Scrupulous: Spiritual Practices, Critical Beliefs, Helpful Prayers
Copyright © 2025 Thomas M. Santa

ISBN 978-0-7648-2875-1
E-ISBN: 978-0-7648-7259-4

Library of Congress Cataloging-in-Publication Data

Names: Santa, Thomas M., 1952- author.
Title: A guide for the scrupulous : spiritual practices, critical beliefs, helpful prayers / Thomas M Santa.
Description: First edition. | Liguori, MO : Liguori Publications, 2025. | Includes bibliographical references. | Summary: "This book presents helpful spiritual practices and prayers from Christian scripture, Catholic saints, and Catholic theologians for people with the religious manifestation of scrupulosity, which is a type of OCD, or obsessive compulsive disorder. Also discussed are critical, yet erroneous, beliefs held by scrupulous people that serve to feed their anxiety and fear"-- Provided by publisher.
Identifiers: LCCN 2025009691 (print) | LCCN 2025009692 (ebook)
  ISBN 9780764828751 (paperback) | ISBN 9780764872594 (ebook)
Subjects: LCSH: Scruples--Religious aspects--Catholic Church. |
  Anxiety--Religious aspects--Catholic Church. | Christian life--Catholic authors.
Classification: LCC BJ1278.S37 S258 2025 (print) | LCC BJ1278.S37 (ebook)
  | DDC 241/.042--dc23/eng/20250521
LC record available at https://lccn.loc.gov/2025009691
LC ebook record available at https://lccn.loc.gov/2025009692

All rights reserved. No part of this publication may be reproduced, stored in a retrieval system, or transmitted in any form or by any means—electronic, mechanical, photocopy, recording, or any other—except for brief quotations in printed reviews, without the prior written permission of Liguori Publications.

The Queen's Work: Liguori Publications has revived *The Queen's Work* imprint to support the needs of the people of God who desire a life of greater piety and devotion, and to encourage the positive spiritual energy that is present in the Church today.

Printed in the United States of America
29 28 27 26 25 / 5 4 3 2 1
First Edition

Memorare (Traditional Prayer)

Remember, O most gracious Virgin Mary,
    that never was it known that anyone
    who fled to your protection,
    implored your help, or sought your intercession,
    was left unaided.

Inspired with this confidence,
    I fly to you, O Virgin of virgins, my Mother;
    to you do I come, before you I stand,
    sinful and sorrowful.

O Mother of the Word Incarnate,
    despise not my petitions,
    but in your mercy hear and answer me.

                                        Amen.

Contents

Introduction — 11

Our Blessed Mother — 17

Part 1
Spiritual Practices — 21

Gratefulness of the Heart at Prayer — 25

The Sacramental Words of Absolution — 30

The Pope's Words: The Joy of the Gospel (*Evangelii Gaudium*) — 46

The Power of the Incarnate Word of God — 57

Five Simple Truths Worth Pondering — 62

An Integrated Spiritual Context for the Scrupulous — 69

Abundant Grace — 83

The Parable of the Prodigal Son — 88

A Fondness for Excess — 92

The Unreflective Life — 97

Part 2
Critical Beliefs 103

I am helpless, caught in a never-ending spiral of emotion, guilt, and anxiety.	107
I am taking advantage of God's love and mercy for me.	113
Scrupulosity is demanding. There are so many rules and rituals that must be followed perfectly.	119
I am the only person who understands my experience of scrupulosity.	123
Mortal sin is like the bogeyman, waiting for me around every corner.	128
Priests do not understand me.	133
Only people with scrupulosity experience unwanted thoughts and feelings, everyone else is normal.	137
I have only one question, and when I get an answer, I will be just fine.	142
God wants me to suffer with scrupulosity. It is the cross that I am supposed to bear.	144
I have sinned so much in life that there is nothing and no one who can make me whole again.	149

Part 3
Helpful Prayers 153

Meditations on the Eucharist by Saint Alphonsus Liguori	156
Helpful Prayers From Various Religious Traditions	181
A Practical Model for Entering Into Prayer	198
Favorite Scripture Passages for Prayer	200
An Eight-Day Retreat Based on Christian Scripture	203

Praying with Ten Companions and Mentors 206

Saint Alphonsus Liguori, CSsR	208
Saint Gerard Majella, CSsR	213
Saint Thérèse of Lisieux	217
Saint Catherine of Siena	221
Saint Hildegard of Bingen	224
Meister Eckhart	228
Saint Teresa of Calcutta	232
Saint Teresa of Ávila	236
Thomas Merton, OCSO	240
C.S. Lewis	244

Notes From the Author	249
Bibliography	253
About the Author	256

"These perspectives will appear absurd to those who don't see that life is, from its origins, groping, adventurous, and dangerous. But these perspectives will grow, like an irresistible idea on the horizon of new generations."

Teilhard de Chardin, SJ

Introduction

I have looked forward to sharing this book with you for a very long time. Despite my anticipation, it was not until recently that I believed the right time had come. It is my hope that what I have collected here will fulfill some of the real spiritual needs of those who suffer with the affliction of scrupulosity.

I wrote this book with the encouragement of numerous men and women with whom I have enjoyed the privilege of spending time during retreats, in conversations, and often through correspondence via the *Scrupulous Anonymous* newsletter and website (**scrupulousanonymous.org**). Their heartfelt concerns and desire to feel more connected to the experience of the sacred has encouraged me. I am very grateful for their participation and suggestions. The dialogue and shared learning experienced on the *Managing Scrupulosity* website (**managingscrupulosity.com**) has also contributed to the wisdom collected here.

You will undoubtedly recognize that many of the reflections included here were originally topics in the monthly *Scrupulous Anonymous* newsletter. I have expanded the previous presentations and included additional thoughts and reflections. In a book, I have freedom to elaborate further on ideas when I feel it will serve the topic well.

I do not pretend that this book will meet all the special needs and requirements of each one of you. Some will discover just enough inspiration and encouragement in these pages. Others may be disappointed because I do not provide satisfactory answers to the questions that are a part of the suffering of scrupulosity. Attempting to answer persistent and unrelenting questions about scrupulosity is not my primary intention with this work. My previous book, **Understanding Scrupulosity**, serves this function and may be helpful. In this book, I offer reflections intended to support your prayer experience and anchor it more firmly in the experience of God's grace and blessing.

Any book intended to help another person pray is,

Introduction

in some sense, presumptuous. After all, how can anyone truly know another's stirrings and yearnings of the heart at prayer with the Lord? Nonetheless, there are some shared experiences and feelings that are part of scrupulosity and, in some instances, present a significant obstacle to prayer. It is my hope that identifying some of these shared obstacles to prayer and offering a new perspective might provide just enough encouragement when it is most needed. I have gathered these reflections in the section titled "Critical Beliefs."

Traditional and orthodox spirituality is not an experience that takes place in a vacuum. All spiritual practice, regardless of the tradition it reflects, flows from the experience of the men and women who have prayed and asked for spiritual help and blessing. In addition to those who repeat historical practices today, we anticipate a future in which these spiritual practices will also be engaged. Spiritual practice is part of a process that includes the individual's capacity for prayer and ability to engage in the required discipline. People with the scrupulous affliction require some specific support and encouragement to increase their capacity to engage in spiritual practice.

In our Catholic tradition, asking for the help and

guidance of our Blessed Mother is most appropriate. The Blessed Mother, specifically called upon in prayer as "Mary, Hope of Sinners," has provided comfort and support for many people. This particular emphasis and devotion are also rooted in Redemptorist tradition and the spirituality of St. Alphonsus Liguori, who is the patron of Scrupulous Anonymous. In his *Glories of Mary*, we read this heartfelt prayer:

> *Most holy, immaculate Virgin and my Mother Mary! To thee who art the Mother of my Lord, the Queen of the world, the Advocate, the Hope, and the Refuge of sinners.*

In addition to the guidance provided by St. Alphonsus and the patronage of our Blessed Mother, this book specifically offers guidance for those men and women who, when called to prayer, do not know what to say or do. On these occasions, it is often helpful to have some trusted prayer starters, meditations, and reflections close at hand. Often, a single thought, word, or experience is all it takes for everything to fall into place. Certain traditional prayers and helpful mentors for prayer seem to be particularly appropriate for people with scrupulosity.

Some readers may be disappointed that specific

Introduction

prayers useful for celebrating the sacrament of reconciliation are not included here. I deliberately omitted them, as there are numerous other books that provide such reflection. I made the pastoral decision that additional commentary on the sacrament of reconciliation is not necessary in this book, as its focus is on expanding the prayer experience and its specific applications to scrupulosity.

First, it is my hope that this book will be pastorally sensitive to your experience and useful for your prayer. What I have written includes both my experience and yours, for a good pastor not only teaches but also listens and learns from the people of God. Second, I pray this book is useful and will become a prayer companion for you both daily and when you need it most. I would be pleased to find this book bent and torn from frequent use, dotted with the occasional stain and filled with holy cards and clippings, because I would know that you used the book for prayer instead of simply finding a home for it on your bookshelf.

As always, let us remember to pray for each other. No one fully understands the power of prayer. Nevertheless, we know that without prayer, there would be something essential missing from our lives. To pray not just for ourselves but for others as well, especially those who suffer with the same affliction, is an invitation of grace and a manifestation of the Word of God, active and alive in our world and in our lives.

Rev. Thomas M. Santa, CSsR
Director, Scrupulous Anonymous

Our Blessed Mother

The story of the wedding feast at Cana has always been one of my favorite biblical stories. Although some biblical commentators suggest it should not be taken at face value, I prefer not to get caught up in those kinds of details. I interpret it as a story that speaks of the intimacy between a mother and a son. Reading it, I see in the exchange between Jesus and the Blessed Mother an illustration of their relationship.

Our Blessed Lady knew she could call upon her Son, and he would respond. It is not primarily the knowledge of his divinity that drove her but rather her knowledge of Jesus as a person. It was Mary who had taught him what it meant to be a human person. It was at her knee that Jesus had learned about respect, obedience, and love. Mary knew her Son was a man who understood the meaning of love, what it meant to be in need, what it meant to be potentially embarrassed. She was confident in her statement: "They have no wine" (John 2:3). She was certain Jesus would respond in a way that was both right and generous, lessening the couple's embarrassment and refocusing the guests' attention. Mary knew Jesus, and because of that, she was able to ask.

As a young boy, I grew up in difficult circumstances. My father abandoned my two sisters and me when we were very young. My mother, who understood that her vocation in life was to be a wife and a mother, was confronted with the fact that she would not realize her dreams—she would be a mother, but not a wife. I can recall many times when I witnessed the consequences of this change in life, especially those consequences that profoundly affected my mother.

As I look back on those days, I remember even more that I was loved. I knew that every decision my mother made, no matter how difficult, was because she believed it was the best for us. Again and again, she chose her children, putting her own life and dreams on the back burner.

I remember one day when I discovered my mother

Introduction

crying on the basement steps. I was unsure of what to do. Children do not expect to see their parents in pain. Nevertheless, there I was. She was not crying about her state of life or her unfulfilled dreams. She was not crying about her own needs or desires. She was crying about us, thinking that somehow she had failed us, that she was not the person she should be. Her tears had nothing to do with herself but everything to do with us, her children.

Later, my mother would always end conversations with the reminder, "Remember to stay close to the Blessed Mother." When I first heard her say this, I simply wrote it off as an expression of her strong and constant devotion to Mary. Now, however, there seems to be more to unpack. Perhaps my mother's reminder to remain close to the Blessed Mother was a reminder to maintain the relationship between mother and son. Perhaps it was intended as a reminder of our struggles and difficulties of growing up. Perhaps it was a reminder that many people, despite their best intentions, do not end up with lives reflective of their desires. Rather, they are presented with different choices, different paths, and it is in these that they discover their vocations and experience of the kingdom of

God. Perhaps it is a reminder to be gentle, accepting, patient, and kind.

I recall all of this when I hear the story of the wedding feast at Cana. The biblical scholars can tell us what it means and symbolizes. I prefer to think of the story as an expression of the intimacy between a mother and her son. Who knows what Jesus felt, or what memory stirred deep within the Lord, when the Blessed Mother told him, "They have no wine."

On June 27 each year, we celebrate the great feast of Our Mother of Perpetual Help. People around the world remember and celebrate our Blessed Mother under this title. She is celebrated in a special way by Redemptorists and the extended Redemptorist family. It is my prayer that those who use this book and their families be blessed in a special way during the month of June. In the words that the priest prays during the novena to Our Mother of Perpetual Help, "May the Lord Jesus Christ be with you, that he may defend you, within you that he may sustain you, before you that he may lead you, behind you that he may protect you, and above you that he may bless you."

Part 1

SPIRITUAL PRACTICES

Within Roman Catholicism, there are many spiritual practices that have been used throughout the centuries. Each spiritual practice has undoubtedly been a source of hope, inspiration, and grace for the person who engages in it. However, for many people who suffer with scrupulosity, the same spiritual practices are often a burden and not necessarily helpful or joyful. This is one of the deepest sufferings experienced by people with scrupulosity—not only are they seemingly cut off from a positive experience with God, but they also seem to be excluded from their own spiritual tradition!

Yes, there are spiritual traditions that people who do not have scrupulosity participate in, and which are not necessarily helpful for the scrupulous. Specifically, the examination of conscience is often an experience of great suffering, is not helpful, and should probably be abandoned by the scrupulous. At the same time, many spiritual traditions are still frequently practiced and are quite useful. However, a specific scrupulous perspective needs to be applied to them. The reflections that follow are my attempt at providing such a perspective, which I hope will be useful and pastorally sensitive.

When appropriate, each of the reflections and spiritual practices that follow are introduced by a traditional prayer to our Blessed Mother. When such a prayer is not provided, another traditional prayer is suggested that helps focus the readers' thoughts on the reflection that follows. It would be helpful to begin your meditative reading by first praying the prayer and then waiting for a moment in anticipation of the reception of the particular grace you have asked for. After a few moments of prayer, your engagement with the following reflection will be appropriate and useful.

PART 1: SPIRITUAL PRACTICES

Gratefulness of the Heart at Prayer

Queen of Heaven, rejoice, alleluia. The Son whom it was your privilege to bear, alleluia, has risen as he promised, alleluia. Pray for us to God, alleluia. Rejoice and be glad, Virgin Mary, alleluia. For the Lord has truly risen, alleluia.

REFLECTION: A close friend of mine shared with me one of his spiritual practices, and it's something each person can easily incorporate into his or her everyday routine. After an initial effort, it becomes easier and quite sustainable. His spiritual practice is this: before going to bed each night, he takes a few moments and identifies three people, events, or experiences from the day for which he is most grateful. As he makes each identification, he simply says, "Thank you, God, for this blessing and this grace." On some days, it may take very little effort to identify those graces and blessings, while on others, a little more effort or creativity may be required. Regardless, it is always worth the effort.

This spiritual practice underlines and brings to individual awareness the awesome power of God's grace and blessing that is alive and at work in our world. Sometimes, because we get caught up in the routine and ordinariness of each day, we might not take the time to notice the presence of God's grace. Because we don't notice or acknowledge it doesn't mean that it is not present. Rather, we may not always enjoy the fullness of the grace and blessings we experience. The fullness of grace comes to us only when we acknowledge and accept gratefully every gift from God. Gratefulness allows even more grace and blessing into our lives as we grow in awareness of the love and care which surrounds us.

Expressing your individual gratefulness for blessings each day is a good practice for all people, but is especially appropriate for those who suffer with scrupulosity. This spiritual practice may balance some of the negativity and anxiety that is so much a part of the experience of scrupulosity. Scrupulosity makes a person hyperaware of what may be wrong, what is lacking, what is incomplete, and what is potentially sinful. If this is your daily experience, then perhaps a healthy helping of gratefulness may be a very real blessing.

If you decide to incorporate this spiritual exercise into your daily discipline, it may be helpful to spend a

PART 1: SPIRITUAL PRACTICES

few moments identifying the people, events, and experiences in your life that are routinely conduits of God's grace for you. This first step is very easy to engage in and often leads to a growing awareness of blessedness that you may have taken for granted. By recalling such moments and manifestations of grace in a manner that is both deliberate and revelatory, you heighten your awareness and appreciation for those moments of grace that are unexpected and out of the ordinary.

You might also take the positive step of examining your experience of scrupulosity to determine if there is any part that is possibly filled with grace. You may look at your present experience of scrupulosity, try to put it into perspective and ask yourself if you can identify any positive improvement. For example, there may be a particular set of circumstances, an unwelcome thought, or an intrusive distraction that you now sense is accompanied by a little less anxiety, a little less fear. This experience of a "little less" can be something you are grateful for and might recognize as a moment of grace and blessing.

During a scrupulous retreat, a gentleman I have known for many years shared with the group that he had finally reached a sustained period in his life where certain thoughts and desires no longer wreaked the spiritual havoc on him they once did. It was only when he was able to examine the spiritual and emotional progress he had made over the years, because of an honest appraisal of his scrupulosity, that he could clearly identify the graces and blessings he now enjoyed. He was pleased because it was something he never expected or thought possible.

A woman once shared with me that she often gave thanks to God that she was able to have the guidance and support of a regular confessor over many years of struggle. She realized there were many people who had never experienced such a blessing. Although she continued to struggle with her scrupulosity, she was nevertheless grateful she did not struggle alone. This was a grace she was able to identify and be thankful for.

Another woman shared in a letter that she had struggled with scrupulosity for many years and expressed thanks and gratefulness for the ministry of Scrupulous Anonymous. For years, she received the newsletter but was unable to contribute to the cost of the production. However, her economic situation changed and she was able to contribute to the costs of production, passing it on to a new generation who might find themselves in the same circumstances she once experienced. She recognized this was a grace and a blessing for her.

In my experience of growing in gratefulness, once I take the time to pay attention to the graces and blessings I receive, I soon realize I am blessed in a manner I did not expect. It is easy to identify events and experiences that are lacking or that prove to be disappointing. On the other hand, recognizing blessings and graces requires more positive effort to make those experiences a constant reality of life.

The spiritual practice of gratefulness of the heart is well worth our effort. This practice manifests the blessings of God at work in our lives, in our community, and in relationships we may take for granted. With a little effort, we too can join our voices with the countless men and women of faith who pray with our Blessed Mother, "My soul proclaims the greatness of the Lord; my spirit has rejoiced in God my savior" (Luke 1:46–47).

The Sacramental Words of Absolution

God, the Father of mercies, through the death and resurrection of his Son has reconciled the world to himself and sent the Holy Spirit among us for the forgiveness of sins; through the ministry of the Church, may God give you pardon and peace, and I absolve you from your sins in the name of the Father, and of the Son, and of the Holy Spirit. Amen. (Traditional)

God, the Father of mercies, through the death and resurrection of his Son, has reconciled the world to himself and poured out the Holy Spirit for the forgiveness of sins; through the ministry of the Church, may God grant you pardon and peace, and I absolve you from your sins in the name of the Father, and of the Son, and of the Holy Spirit. Amen. (Revised)

REFLECTION: The sacramental words of absolution prayed by the priest in the sacrament of reconciliation invite meditation and reflection. Unfortunately, because of the anxiety many people feel in the confessional, they cannot fully appreciate the power of these words and the amazing grace these words proclaim. This reflection may help you appreciate this sacramental encounter with the person of Jesus. The prayer is divided into distinct parts, with a point of reflection for each section.

God, the Father of mercies, through the death and resurrection of his Son...

These words represent the revelation of Jesus and his personal relationship with his heavenly Father, his Abba. This revelation is central to our understanding of what it means to truly celebrate Jesus' healing power when we encounter the Lord under the sacramental sign.

For a Jew of the first century, the idea that the God of the Old Testament might be embraced as Abba was entirely beyond belief. The God of the Old Testament was the all-powerful Creator-God who demanded that his people remain faithful to him.

The primary interpreters of the relationship between Yahweh and his people insisted that he could best be obeyed by careful observance of each of the rules and tenets of the Law of Moses. Those who broke the law risked alienation, not only from God, but also from the community of believers. This alienation was tantamount to death, because no one could imagine how life could continue without the support of the community, family, and friends.

In this context and prevailing attitude, Jesus waded into the experience and turned it upside down. Without dismissing either the law or the spiritual practices determined by it, he invited his followers to an entirely different experience of God. Experiencing God in this new way consisted of three steps: 1) personal truthfulness, 2) a sense of vulnerability, and 3) an experience of profound intimacy and relationship. Jesus invited his followers to perceive their world, community, and relationships as manifestations of the kingdom of God.

It wasn't easy then, nor is it now, to accept his invitation. To embrace the kingdom of God and grow in personal relationship with Abba, each person must lose his or her life in order to save it (see Matthew 16:25 or Luke 17:33). In other words, each individual learns to let go of the old ways of living, judging, perceiving, loving, and forgiving that are anchored in the fears and anxieties of not measuring up and being less than perfect.

PART 1: SPIRITUAL PRACTICES

Jesus fundamentally invites us to embrace something that comes purely as gift, as grace from God.

The first step is to learn to be as truthful as possible about yourself, your relationships, your thoughts and desires, and your real needs and expectations. Sometimes, this is very pleasant and freeing; for example, when you correctly identify your personal gifts and talents. This process can also be painful when you recognize your faults and failings and accept that you are not always as loving or wonderful as you imagine yourself to be.

Only when you have achieved the first step can you take the second step: acceptance. When you accept that which is most true and authentic about yourself and take personal responsibility for your thoughts, words, and actions, you become vulnerable to yourself, others, and, ultimately, to God. It is hard to admit and accept something painful that fills you with doubt and anxiety. But there is great power and grace in this vulnerability when you are able to embrace it and continue living in hope and the expectation of God's grace and concern.

The third step (and there is no shortcut), is to grow in your relationship with Abba, the Father, because you know you are loved and beloved—not as you one day might be, but exactly as you are in this moment. The intimacy of the experience is powerful because to know and experience that you are loved—warts and all—is ultimately freeing and life-giving.

When Jesus reveals his truth—that Abba is a God and Father of mercy, not of judgment and condemnation—he invites us into a completely different way of perceiving and experiencing our world. When Jesus stands in the ultimate position of vulnerability—first in his agony in the garden and then dramatically before Pilate and his accusers—he is powerless. He is perceived to have failed in his mission. To outsiders, he hadn't changed hearts or perceptions, and his fate had been determined. The kingdom was seen as lost, and the old way of seeing and believing had triumphed once again. Jesus poured out everything, and it was not enough—or so it seemed.

Only after everything was stripped away and poured out with nothing left was the true love of Abba, the Father, revealed. God hadn't abandoned Jesus, but rather he imagined something more, something beyond comprehension, something to be revealed as the final answer to those who refused to believe, to see, and to live in the light of the kingdom of God.

PART 1: SPIRITUAL PRACTICES

The experience of resurrection is his final answer. There is no separation and no alienation, and all is and always made whole and complete through the power of the grace of God made manifest.

The opening words of our prayer of absolution remind us that through Jesus' death and resurrection, the ultimate truth about his Abba is revealed. They invite us to recall that life is a journey made up of many experiences, each graced by God in some way. The words of absolution remind us that the same grace which was active in Jesus' life—in the good and difficult moments—is also active in our lives.

We are not alone. We are not isolated. We are not alienated. We are not singled out for judgment or punishment. The words of absolution are words of hope and praise, not of condemnation. They set the celebratory tone of the sacramental experience as an encounter with the living God, who is always active and alive in us.

Our heavenly Father, revealed to us as the all-loving Abba, is a Father of mercy. He is with us in all the moments of our lives, including death, calling us forth into the resurrection, the experience of Jesus—our Way, our Truth, and our Life.

...has reconciled the world to himself and poured out the Holy Spirit for the forgiveness of sins...

Notice that the priest isn't praying these words in hope or anticipation that the world will be reconciled; rather, he is proclaiming that the world has been reconciled. Jesus' Incarnation and saving passion, death, and resurrection removed even the hint of separation and alienation between humanity and our heavenly Father. The great chasm—the rupture in our relationship caused by sin—was forever healed, repaired, and restored permanently through Jesus.

There may be some lingering sense of alienation or separation between a person and God, but there is no actual separation. No alienation exists and no separation is possible.

We can state this wonderful fact with all assurance and conviction, not because of any merits we have earned but because of the presence of the Holy Spirit of God. Through the Spirit of God, the guarantee of reconciliation is perfectly proclaimed and realized. The Spirit, sent by Jesus after his resurrection, gives us this sacred comfort and path of wisdom, the fortifier of God's grace at work.

PART 1: SPIRITUAL PRACTICES

The presence of the Holy Spirit proclaims the reconciliation of humankind with the Creator-God, our Abba. No action, event, or experience is required to ensure this heavenly gift of grace.

In response to God's grace and the Holy Spirit's presence, we become instruments of God's reconciling spirit. Through our thoughts, words, and actions, the people of God manifest the reconciliation given and graced to us by Jesus' Incarnation. When we know we have been reconciled to our heavenly Father, we choose to put into action the grace of trying our best to live as the children of God. As Matthew 18:21–22 states, "'Lord, if my brother sins against me, how often must I forgive him? As many as seven times?' Jesus answered, 'I say to you, not seven times but seventy-seven times.'"

The reconciling grace of God, given to each person daily by the Spirit of God in our midst, cannot be measured or parceled out and is never in short supply. God's gift of grace is abundant in the world. Each time we become instruments of this grace, we confirm the presence of the Holy Spirit in our lives.

The abundance of God's grace guaranteed by the Holy Spirit stands in sharp contrast to the perception of forgiveness experienced by some people: forgiveness must be earned and is in short supply. To feel that grace is not abundant, that it is conditional or in danger of running out, is a serious temptation against the Spirit of God. It is the "blindness" of the scribes and Pharisees, who were in constant conflict with Jesus whenever he spoke about the kingdom of God.

When people struggle to name every sin and every possible nuance or feeling that may or may not have accompanied what they perceive as sin, they feel a scarcity of grace and dread of mortal sin; they feel that any error, anything less than perfection, will result in the denial of forgiveness and grace. They may think the heavenly Father is dangling the gift of forgiveness in front of them, tantalizingly close, ready to snatch it away at any moment.

There is cruelty in this perception, a never-ending sense of dread, incompleteness, and emptiness that can never be satisfied, no matter how we respond. With this skewed perception, every response will be incomplete, imperfect, and in direct contrast to the pervading reality of the presence of God's grace and the Holy Spirit, which is never to be denied or removed.

As we grow in relationship with God, we learn to embrace truthfulness, acknowledge vulnerability, and

PART 1: SPIRITUAL PRACTICES

experience the intimacy of our relationship with him, ultimately discovering how gifted and blessed we are.

When people encounter this truth, they want to believe it. They long to be freed from their incorrect perception of somehow being separated from God, but they fear it will become a reality. This is one horrific consequence of scrupulosity, a.k.a. the "doubting disease." It robs us of the peace of knowing we are loved and beloved, and it prevents us from experiencing the abundance of God's grace and life.

Acknowledging that this feeling is the result of the disease and not the reality of our relationship with God is the grace we must pray for. We must come face-to-face with vulnerability and learn to accept it while refusing to let it dominate our thoughts and feelings.

...through the ministry of the Church, may God grant you pardon and peace...

We are direct instruments of God's grace and blessing when we act in his name, becoming a source of blessing and encouragement for one another. When the priest acknowledges in his prayer that the Church—which includes all of God's people—is responding to

God's grace and sharing God's blessings, he gives praise and thanks to God for the gift of the Spirit. Our actions are indeed the gift of the Spirit, as the Apostle Paul taught: "In him we live and move and have our being" (Acts 17:28). Grace is the animating spirit of the people of God. Because of grace, all our thoughts and actions in response to this gift are an act of ministry, the gift of the Spirit of God.

In union with the ministry of the Church, the sacrament of reconciliation bestows the pardon and peace of God on those who receive this special grace. We cannot be separated from God; our reconciliation has been completed through the sacrifice of Jesus. This reality should reassure us and settle our restless hearts.

God's pardon and peace also need to be experienced by the individual. The effective ministry of reconciliation—the peace and pardon of God—comes from God, but it also depends on each of us. Each person who receives and accepts the grace of reconciliation must respond to the gift of grace by living as a person who believes he or she is reconciled to God.

Those who confirm the reconciliation by their thoughts and actions are essential ministers of God's healing and reconciliation. Reconciliation would be

PART 1: SPIRITUAL PRACTICES

incomplete if pardon and peace came only from God and was not experienced by each of us. This is the great gesture of reconciliation, the sanctifying grace of the sacrament, but it is also a place of unresolved conflict and other feelings.

Through the sacramental grace we receive, we are invited to cooperate with God's grace—to accept and practice what it means to be pardoned of our sinfulness and be filled with God's peace. When the priest prays the prayer of absolution, he reflects God's grace at work in the world and expresses the hope that the people of God will accept this grace and choose to manifest the power of the reconciliation in their thoughts, words, and actions. The fullness of the grace of reconciliation is incomplete if it is not gratefully received and shared. God's word is intended to be listened to and always put into practice.

This dynamic is often difficult for people to embrace, especially those who are tempted to confess past sins repeatedly because of fear, anxiety, or some sense of incompleteness or imperfection. Although it is not sinful by any stretch of the imagination, the inability to believe fully and completely in God's pardon and peace has consequences.

The most obvious consequence is the inability to be sustained and comforted in knowing we have received the complete gift of reconciliation. When we don't feel reconciled, it's difficult to believe we can be instruments of God's reconciling grace in the world. In fact, we feel like an obstacle to God's grace. This feeling deepens our burden and anxiety, often producing gloom that robs us of happiness and satisfaction.

Sins must not, under any circumstances, be confessed more than once. It is imperative to cooperate with the grace received in the sacrament by accepting that each penitent is granted the fullness of God's pardon and peace.

The power of the grace of the sacrament flows from the abundance of God's love. It is not contingent upon our individual perfection, attention, or ability to fully accept what that grace provides.

...and I absolve you from your sins in the name of the Father, and of the Son, and of the Holy Spirit. Amen.

For older Catholics, these words capture the true meaning of the sacrament. Schooled in the traditions and practices of the Council of Trent, the Catholic ear was trained to hear these words: *"Ego te absolvo"* ("I absolve you."). These words proclaimed to the penitent that the priest, as judge and representative of Christ, had accepted the penitent's confession of sins in number, matter, and kind. The penitent understood that his or her sins had been forgiven. The priest had determined no reason to refuse absolution, and all that was now required was the penitent's dutiful performance of the penance.

The penitent may have felt relief but was also aware of the "temporal punishment due to sin" that hadn't yet been satisfied. Purgatory awaited him or her, but most assuredly the eternal damnation of the fires of hell had been staved off, at least for now, unless he or she had deliberately concealed a mortal sin. In that instance, those same words confirmed the sacrilege of the penitent, which was considered even more damning than a mortal sin and was of course to be avoided.

At this point, the beautiful theology of the prayer of absolution seems to give way to the canonical requirement for the valid dispensation of the sacrament of reconciliation. The words of absolution may appear cold and sterile, but perhaps that is unavoidable because they were originally intended as a "sentence of the law."

This is why many people dread confession and penance. Who among us doesn't feel anxiety and dread when we're judged, even when innocent? When the Second Vatican Council renewed the liturgy and ritual of each sacrament, it also addressed the anxiety associated with the sacrament of reconciliation by changing the sacrament's emphasis to its healing nature and the power of God's grace.

Catechetical teaching about this new emphasis was enthusiastically embraced, but some may still remember the emphasis of the older theology. For them, the words, "I absolve you from your sins" suggest that the priest remains the judge and that a standard must be met. The law seems to confirm this viewpoint for anyone who feels the anxiety of the sacrament instead of the joy of reconciliation. This is unfortunate but understandable.

For many people, the pronouncement of the words of absolution signals the end of the formal ritual of the sacrament, but it doesn't necessarily end their anxiety, questioning, and constant rumination over sin. It is better to consciously dwell on the rest of the prayer instead. In this way, some of the dread and uncertainty might be redirected from feelings of judgment to the beauty of the sacrament and the grace that has been received.

I hope this reflection about the beautiful prayer of absolution has deepened and expanded your appreciation for the power of the prayer and enabled you to understand it within a theological context of redemption and mercy, with less emphasis on the required canonical words and more emphasis on the entire prayer. As a priest-confessor, I am aware of my canonical responsibilities when I pray this prayer for you, but I am all the more inspired and encouraged when I fully appreciate and understand the entire prayer as a proclamation of God's grace and life at work in the world.

The Pope's Words: The Joy of the Gospel (*Evangelii Gaudium*)

O Mary, direct and influence my life as you did in the early days of the Church. I need your care and love as much as the apostles, saints, and confessors of old. Be a Mother to me, as to them. O Mary, I thank you. Mary, Mother of the Church, pray for me.

REFLECTION: Early in his papacy, Pope Francis released a document to the universal Church that is classified as an exhortation. This type of papal document is a form of communication from the pope to the Church, intended to encourage and enlighten. Exhortations are not orientated toward doctrine or classified to be as influential as a papal encyclical, but they are nevertheless important for the life of the Church. Generally, a papal exhortation is issued at the conclusion of a Synod of Bishops. This particular exhortation was issued in partial response to the October 2012 Synod of Bishops.

The Joy of the Gospel speaks primarily about the new evangelization, the missionary transformation of the

PART 1: SPIRITUAL PRACTICES

Church, and the challenges of today's world, all within the context of exhorting the people of God to find joy in the gospel. It is a challenging and inspirational exhortation worthy of prayer and reflection. Those who struggle with scrupulosity may find the section titled "A Mission Embodied Within Human Limits" very encouraging and reassuring. The following comes from that section:

"I want to remind priests that the confessional must not be a torture chamber but rather an encounter with the Lord's mercy which spurs us on to do our best. A small step, in the midst of great human limitations, can be more pleasing to God than a life which appears outwardly in order but moves through the day without confronting great difficulties. Everyone needs to be touched by the comfort and attraction of God's saving love, which is mysteriously at work in each person, above and beyond their faults and failings" (*Evangelii Gaudium,* 44).

This paragraph reminds me of each of you. How reassuring it is to hear such words of encouragement. These words speak of Pope Francis' pastoral heart, his sense of what the people of God often struggled with. I believe his feelings about this matter were not the result of lofty academic pursuit but rather of his personal experience in the confessional, when he listened to the people who came to the sacrament to receive God's grace. It is quite reasonable to believe that some individuals who sought his support and guidance struggled with scrupulosity. These words reflect this reality in the life of the Pope and in those he has served. We will reflect upon three distinct points from *The Joy of the Gospel.*

First, Pope Francis acknowledged that the experience of confession can often be very painful or even excruciating. Each of us knows this feeling, this pain. It is not that we seek misery or suffering, but it is the result of the debilitating effects of obsession, compulsion, and ritual that play out within the sacrament. Scrupulous people do not choose to suffer in this manner; rather, their illness compels the suffering to come full circle. A short period of relief results from the ritual of confession but is soon replaced with even more doubting, anxiety, and frustration as the cycle continues and repeats itself, with no evident end in sight.

Second, Pope Francis acknowledged that with such an experience, what we should reasonably hope for is not some dramatic change but rather a "small step," indicating that he comprehended that the effort spent

PART 1: SPIRITUAL PRACTICES

by the scrupulous penitent—the emotion and suffering endured—is not rewarded proportionally within the experience of the sacrament. Usually, when a person expends a significant amount of energy on something, he or she experiences a measurable return. For the scrupulous individual, all of his or her energy is consumed by the repeated scrupulous ritual of confession, doubting, anxiety, and questioning. There is no sense of sustained relief or accomplishment, no sense of pleasing God or self. There is continuously more of the same. Pope Francis reassured the scrupulous penitent that the smallest step is pleasing to God. In other words, the confession of sins does not have to be perfect, complete, or exhaustive—the effort itself is pleasing to God!

Third, Pope Francis recognized that scrupulosity is a burden that is carried all day, every day. It is frequently unnoticed by those with whom scrupulous people associate, but it is nonetheless very real. The Pope understood that it is a "great difficulty" and robs the person of the experience of knowing that he or she is loved by God. Scrupulosity turns the smallest defect, sin, or failing into a heavy load that the scrupulous person must carry. It exaggerates the effects of sin and encourages the false belief that a person is somehow cut off and permanently barred from the fullness of experiencing God's grace. In *The Joy of the Gospel*, Pope Francis tried to offer another perception by assuring each of us that we are in fact loved by God in ways we cannot even begin to imagine.

In his introductory remarks, Pope Francis wrote some words that are appropriate to consider at this point in our reflection:

"God never tires of forgiving us; we are the ones who tire of seeking his mercy.... No one can strip us of the dignity bestowed upon us by this boundless and unfailing love. With a tenderness which never disappoints, but is always capable of restoring our joy, he makes it possible for us to lift up our heads and to start anew. Let us not flee from the resurrection of Jesus, let us never give up, come what will" (*EG* 3).

If Pope Francis could have spoken to each person suffering with the scrupulous disorder, I believe he would have assured us that he understood that the burden of scrupulosity is exhausting. So many times, we are tempted to give up, to let feelings of desperation and depression overwhelm us. In times such as these, we must remind ourselves of Pope Francis' words and hold on to the conviction that the Lord has not abandoned us. We may not feel his love or concern for us, but his grace and life are nevertheless a reality in our lives. The Lord invites us to "lift up our heads" and to believe we are loved and forgiven by him. The illness and manifestation of scrupulosity may attempt to strip a person of his or her dignity as a child of God, but God's grace will never be defeated.

"I realize of course that joy is not expressed the same way at all times in life, especially at moments of great difficulty. Joy adapts and changes, but it always endures, even as a flicker of light born of our personal certainty that, when everything is said and done, we are infinitely loved. I understand the grief of people who have to endure great suffering, yet slowly but surely we all have to let the joy of faith slowly revive as a quiet yet firm trust, even amid the greatest distress" (*EG* 6).

The topic of our next point of consideration is illustrated clearly in a letter I recently received:

"I'm terrified of some things the *Catholic Encyclopedia* says about probabilism and doubt, about how we must be absolutely certain or only take the safest route in some cases. I do, of course, research doubts and questions, but sometimes I panic over things that don't really have an answer or need my own discernment. I'm afraid of tempting a loved one into sin, and I discuss it with the person. The person assures me that he or she doesn't feel the way I feared he or she would, but then I have a scruple over whether I should trust the person or should continue to dig for the presence of objective sin. How certain can we be?"

Hopefully, it is easy to recognize one of the perils of scrupulosity in this question. I repeatedly caution people not to fall into the agonizing trap of attempting to "research their way out" of scrupulosity. This is an impossible task and one of the reasons that professionals have identified scrupulosity as "a thousand frightening fantasies" or "the doubting disease." Every researched answer will immediately be replaced with more questions. There is no certainty possible when someone is in the grips of an obsessive-compulsive ritual that drives and energizes the need for an answer. Even for someone who does not have scrupulosity, this certainty is impossible. The only difference between those who suffer with scrupulosity and those who don't is in the level of comfort: the scrupulous person feels that the uncertainty is indicative of an incomplete effort or less-than-honest discernment, while the non-scrupulous person is more often comfortable with the feeling of being unsure.

The scrupulous person's compulsion for certainty speaks directly to the discussion of imputability and responsibility referenced by the Holy Father in *The Joy of the Gospel*. Quoting the *Catechism of the Catholic Church* (*CCC*), he states that "imputability and responsibility for an action can be diminished or even nullified by ignorance, inadvertence, duress, fear, habit, inordinate attachments, and other psychological or social factors" (*EG* 44). For the scrupulous person, it is most certainly not ignorance or inadvertence that we might define as the point of diminishment of responsibility, but rather duress and fear. I am inclined to state that, often, the duress associated with the fear of sin can be understood as an essential definition of the scrupulous conscience.

In simpler language, my experience has shown that scrupulous people who suffer not with the symptoms of a tender conscience but instead with a religious manifestation of obsessive-compulsive disorder (OCD) are some of the most God-fearing, honest, and responsible people. Their whole lives are defined by their desire to please God and live as faithfully as possible. Unfortunately—and this is the real scourge of scrupulosity—they do not personally believe they are this type of person. In fact, they believe exactly the opposite. They see themselves as great sinners who do not love God and are always trying to wiggle their way out of serious situations and challenges. They do not see themselves as loved but as unloved.

This perception that scrupulous people have about themselves is real. It is not a fantasy; it is the reality of how they experience their everyday lives. They cannot be "talked out" of it. They cannot be presented with enough evidence to the contrary. In short, this perception is real and most likely something they will carry their entire lives. This perception distorts reality—not their perception of reality, but reality itself. This distortion of reality is marked by great fear and duress about sin. In fact, it provides all that is required by the technical definition of moral thought and action to supply them with imputability and responsibility from the full effects of what they fear the most. Interestingly, the very fact that most scrupulous individuals resist accepting that they are not responsible for what they feel provides definitive proof that this distortion of reality applies to them.

PART 1: SPIRITUAL PRACTICES

Perhaps one of the most difficult challenges scrupulous individuals might encounter is learning to accept their limitations—not the limitations they fear they have, but the limitations they actually experience. There is a distinct difference. Scrupulous people fear that they are terrible sinners, incapable of being loved and forgiven unless they are always diligent in resisting and overcoming sin. This perception limits them and presents the challenges with which they are faced. Scrupulous people must learn to patiently accept that their disease limits their ability to think well of themselves and accept God's love. They must also patiently learn about their distinct fears and the emotions that accompany such fears, especially in regard to sin. It is perhaps even more difficult for them to learn to accept the reality of their limitations not as God's punishment but as a direct result of their illness.

These limitations are not impossible to manage. Pope Francis teaches a central truth that we need to hear and accept: "The Eucharist, although it is the fullness of sacramental life, is not a prize for the perfect but a powerful medicine and nourishment for the weak" (*EG* 47). In other words, as scrupulous people struggle with the limitations imposed by their illness, they need not, and should not, deprive themselves of the Eucharist because of their fears and struggles. This is often a strong temptation, but it should be resisted because it unnecessarily deprives them of the spiritual remedy and medicine they need the most.

Remember: "A small step, in the midst of great human limitations, can be more pleasing to God than a life which appears outwardly in order but moves through the day without confronting great difficulties" (*EG* 44). All of us are capable of small steps, and it is reassuring to be reminded that each small step is very pleasing to the Lord.

PART 1: SPIRITUAL PRACTICES

The Power of the Incarnate Word of God

Each year, in December, the Church celebrates the liturgical season of Advent. In our liturgical celebrations, our personal prayer, and even the secular decorations of the season, people of faith are invited to focus on one event: what happened at the stable in Bethlehem so many centuries ago. In this unique historical moment, Jesus, the Son of God, became for us the Word made flesh and dwelt among us. Our attention is focused on this specific moment in time because it helps us celebrate a uniquely Christian event: the Incarnation.

This special time of year celebrates the fact that the Word of God became a human being. This reality is not the uniquely Christian part of the event. In ancient pagan religions, other gods became flesh, and, as a result, the Christian assertion does not stand alone. For example, most of the Greek and Roman gods took on human flesh. Such gods coupled with humans to produce offspring that was half human, half god. Still others assumed human forms to cause mischief or test human beings in some kind of competition. Therefore, the proclamation of the Christian God becoming human is not unique. However, the reason for it is.

The ancient pagan gods became human to play with, trick, or punish humanity. They became human for their own purposes and pleasures. Never did these dead gods truly "empty themselves" or let go of their true nature. Their assumed humanity was used as a shield or distraction so they could wreak havoc and mischief. This is not the Christian belief we hold. This distinction invites us to truly embrace and celebrate the uniquely Christian component that molds our faith.

Jesus did not become a human being to play or frolic. He did not become a human being for his own pleasure, and his humanity was not a shield for his divinity. As Christians, we proclaim that Jesus became a human being because he was sent by his Father into the world to redeem the people of God—to set us free and to become for us our salvation. He became incarnate "So that the Father may see and love in us what he has seen and loved in his Son" (*Roman Missal, Preface VII*).

Jesus became a human being to cement the relationship finally and completely between God and humanity. This relationship of intimacy, shared responsibility, and co-creation was promised to God's people through God's covenant with Abraham. This is a uniquely Christian belief and is what we celebrate in all its wonder and glory. Every Christmas tree, cookie, and present, each in its own way, is part of what we hold in faith to be true. Each event and experience leading up to the feast of Christmas, and Christmas Day itself, are meant to help us come to a deeper and more profound appreciation of what it means for us when we proclaim that Jesus became a human person.

Thomas Merton, the well-known Trappist monk, wrote in his book *The New Seeds of Contemplation:*

> *As a magnifying glass concentrates the rays of the sun into a little burning knot of heat that can set fire to a dry leaf or a piece of paper, so the mysteries of Christ in the gospel concentrate the rays of God's light and fire to a point that sets fire to the spirit of man. And this is why Christ was born and lived in the world and died and returned from death and ascended to his Father in heaven…through the glass of his humanity, he concentrates the rays of his Holy Spirit upon us so that we feel the burn.*

He explains that the Incarnation—the Son of God becoming human—was intended to focus our attention on our relationship with God. The Incarnation provides humanity with an intensity of emotion that was unknown to humanity prior to the coming of Jesus. Neither Abraham nor others from the Old Testament, such as Moses, Jacob, and Esther, understood this type of relationship with God. We experience this new type of relationship because Jesus became human. As such, it changes us, just as the burning knot of heat changes all that it touches.

While the truth of the Incarnation is one that invites all people to ponder and reflect deeply, this type of reflection is most important for those who struggle with scrupulosity. The most essential reflection to contemplate is the contrast between the truth of and reason for the Incarnation versus the pagan stories of mythology mentioned previously. It is crucial to arrive at an understanding and appreciation of the Incarnation as a saving event, one that was intended to draw God's people into an ever-increasing experience of intimacy with God. God does not play with us, nor does he set up tasks and temptations to trip us up or draw us into sin. God desires to be with us, not against us, in the struggle. He is not the source or root of the struggle.

What makes us feel far from God is not the manifestation of the presence of God. It is rather the manifestation of a sickness: the power of scrupulosity to twist, obscure, and confuse our real relationship with God. It is when we feel the most vulnerable, the most unloved, that we need to permit the magnifying glass of the Incarnate Christ to burn away the negative feelings and permit the burn of grace, the burn of the Holy Spirit, to fill us with hope and blessing. Let us pray that we all experience something of the healing intimacy of the unique presence of God at work in our lives.

Five Simple Truths Worth Pondering

I came across these five simple truths and believe they may be helpful for people who suffer with scrupulosity. Although these statements come from an anonymous source, they are from someone who is in touch with the power of God's grace at work in his or her life. These truths were originally titled "Five Quick and Easy Ways to Determine If What You're Hearing Really Has Anything to Do With God."

Number One:
If it produces fear, it does not come from God.

Scripture teaches, "Fear of the LORD is the beginning of knowledge" (Proverbs 1:7). The "fear of the Lord" is understood as one of the seven gifts of the Holy Spirit. Knowing well these reference points from the sacred Scriptures, I would nevertheless assert that this rule is essential for true peace and happiness, even though it appears to contradict Scripture.

When Scripture speaks of "fear of the Lord," it is best understood as assuming a posture of mystery, awe, and wonder when coming face-to-face with the gran-

PART 1: SPIRITUAL PRACTICES

deur and majesty of God. For a person whose routine experience of such grandeur and opulence may have been that of an ancient Near Eastern king or emperor (such as the writer of Proverbs), an attitude of submission in fear and trembling may well have made sense. However, for a person of our time and experience who routinely stands before the splendor of the unfolding universe—which far outshines the magnificence of any king's court—a more reasonable posture is that of awe and wonder.

Fear, on the other hand, such as the fear of punishment, embarrassment, or some other emotion that is not life-giving, is not a manifestation of the power of God. It is rather an emotion that paralyzes or freezes a person into inaction. Fear, as a basic instinct, is a useful impulse when you are faced with something unknown or immediately threatening. However, if your sense of fear is an always-present state of mind, then it becomes numbing and slowly drains away life and grace. God's plan for you does not include numbing fear; God's plan and desire for his people are vibrant and grace-filled lives.

Number Two:
If it is self-diminishing, it does not come from God.

In the first pages of the book of Genesis, we read, "God looked at everything he had made, and found it very good" (Genesis 1:31). In short, the summary of God's opinion about his creation is that he is "well pleased" (Matthew 3:17). These two statements suggest that God celebrates his creation, which includes each one of his people. To diminish a creature of God after the Creator has judged that creature to be good is contradictory and not supported by the Scriptures.

It is possible, and indeed admirable, to give praise and thanks to God for the wonders of his creation. When we are personally praised for a job well done, it is also admirable to sincerely repeat that all the honor and glory belongs to the Lord. Each gesture is possible without diminishing the individual person or the gifts and talents with which the person is blessed. In a very real sense, when we accept praise with a grateful heart, that acceptance in turn gives praise and honor to the God we serve. If, on the other hand, we diminish or minimize the effort of another person, sometimes in a vain attempt to make ourselves look better, that diminishment and debasement is not God's word or judgment about the person's efforts. It is a "false word," an unsettling and unnecessary pronouncement that does not come from God but rather from another source. God builds up and celebrates his people; he does not tear down and diminish either his creation or his creatures.

Number Three:
If it motivates hate, it does not come from God.

The oft-repeated quote, "Hate the sin, but love the sinner," is usually attributed to St. Augustine. However, I do not believe that hate in any form is from God. According to the Merriam-Webster dictionary, the word "hate" comes from the Old English *hete*, and is defined as "intense hostility and aversion, usually stemming from fear, anger, or sense of injury." When people experience hate, they usually use it to cover an enormous range of feelings and situations. For example, you may hear a young child say simple statements such as "I hate broccoli," or "I hate doing homework." On a more serious and realistic level, a leader of a country may attempt to exterminate those of a certain religion or ethnicity because of hate. Hate is often intertwined with other emotions, such as fear or anger, but is distinctly different from them.

It is obvious that the feeling and the expression of hate cannot possibly come from God. To feel hate, or to express some form of hatred, even in casual speech, cannot in any way be understood as an expression of a person who is trying to live a grace-filled life. Hate turned inward, away from other people into the individual self, is even more destructive and damaging.

Number Four:
If it produces shame, it does not come from God.

Shame is a multifaceted emotion. If it is experienced as guilt, regret, or embarrassment because of something you did that you understand was wrong, it is not an uncommon feeling. In small doses, and with a healthy sense of self-awareness and responsibility, it can be a helpful emotion. If, on the other hand, the feeling of shame seems always to be present—not because of something you freely chose to do but rather as a description of how you might perceive and understand yourself as a person ("I am filled with shame")—then this kind of experience is not healthy.

PART 1: SPIRITUAL PRACTICES

Understand and claim as your personal truth that through the power of your baptism and the power of God's grace at work in your life, you have been freed from the enslaving effects of sin. When you stand before the Lord, not because of your own merits but because of God's gifts, you stand before him proudly with your brothers and sisters as a child of God. The sacrifice of Jesus has freed you from the experience and constant condition of shame. Hold your head high, knowing you have been called into life by God and graced with his love.

Number Five:
If it deprives you of freedom, it does not come from God.

The daily struggle with scrupulosity compromises your experience of the freedom that God intends for you. Scrupulosity is not God's will for you. You do not suffer from this disorder because God has singled you out for suffering and punishment. Scrupulosity is a disorder, an emotional and pathological illness that affects certain members of the human family. It is not unlike other illnesses or disorders that are routinely experienced by many men and women. As such, any efforts you might make to control, modify, or even cure yourself of this disorder is not contrary to God's will for you. It is God's will that you are free and that you enjoy the fullest possible freedom as a child of God.

Scrupulosity severely impacts your experience of freedom and your ability to make free and conscious choices in your life. This is one of the reasons that your confessor may often repeat that you have not, by any stretch of the imagination, fulfilled all the requirements for mortal and serious sin, despite what you may perceive and how you may feel. Scrupulosity deprives you of freedom and is a burden you carry.

PART 1: SPIRITUAL PRACTICES

An Integrated Spiritual Context for the Scrupulous

When we speak about spirituality, it is helpful to understand that the experience of being a spiritual person is not tied to a single religious expression or practice. All human beings are spiritual beings, a point well illustrated by the Jesuit priest Pierre Teilhard de Chardin in his classic *The Phenomenon of Man* (1955). In the book, he explains, "We are spiritual beings having human experiences, not human beings having spiritual experiences." With this perspective, we can add an additional insight by stating that spirituality is best understood as a "trans-religious" experience. In other words, just as we can speak about Christian spirituality, we can also speak about Muslim, Jewish, and Hindu spirituality, to name a few.

As Christians, we emphasize specific components of our spiritual tradition as essential. For example, we base our understanding of what it means to be a spiritual person on two root words, one from the Hebrew and one from the Greek. In Hebrew, we use the word *ruach,* and in Greek, we use the word *pneuma,* both of which mean "breath, wind, or spirit," equally applied to both the human and the divine. With this knowledge,

Christians assert that acknowledging our spirituality and becoming aware that we are indeed spiritual beings has something to do with the integration of body, mind, and spirit. We can remind ourselves of St. Paul's teaching in the Acts of the Apostles: "In him we live and move and have our being" (Acts 17:28).

As we continue to review the basic components of growing in awareness of the fact that we are spiritual beings, we begin trying to connect with the spiritual experience of being human people. As such, we look at our experiences, relationships, and practices, assuming that if we are to touch divinity and know something of the sacred, these are the places in which we might encounter a sense of our spiritual lives.

Experience: Spiritual experiences may be dramatic or quite ordinary. Regardless, such experiences bring the human person to a deeper understanding of the sacred in ordinary life—for example, holding a newborn child and realizing that this new, fragile life is a gift from God. Or standing outside at night, looking up into the sky, and becoming aware of the immensity of the universe. For others, the onset of a serious illness or unexpected personal challenge brings them face-to-face with their humanity and the sacred and mysterious.

PART 1: SPIRITUAL PRACTICES

Relationships: Relationships are at the very core of what it means to be a human person. All people experience life as relational, beginning with birth and ending in death. Along the way, we encounter and experience all manner of men, women, and children, each of whom are also on this great journey of life. Some of our relationships will be very positive and life-giving; for example, relationships with people who freely profess their love for us as spouse, father, mother, sibling, friend. Other relationships can be challenging and even painful as we come into an ever-growing awareness that we are fragile, weak, and not as independent as we might wish to be. To know we are not universally loved or appreciated by every person we encounter is a hard lesson to learn and experience.

Practices: Spiritual practices are intentional, specific actions that a person engages in to connect with his or her understanding of the divine, the sacred, and the mysterious. Often, such practices are deeply rooted in a particular culture or specific tradition. Such practices can be easily identified with a particular religious expression; for example, our Catholic understanding and celebration of the Eucharist. Some are understood as essential; for example, the required ritual cleansing or purification before engaging in certain practices. Some are reflective of a communitarian response, while still others are deeply personal and private. It would not be an exaggeration to assert that many spiritual practices are best understood as "heartfelt" and deeply rooted within the individual personality of the one who practices them.

When we understand that spirituality is integrative, we strive to balance our experiences, relationships, and practices in such a way that complement and support us. For example, a spiritual practice that denies a person access to life-giving relationships might be an acceptable path for a monk, but it is most certainly not advantageous for other expressions of human life.

It is very important for those who struggle with scrupulosity to spend some quality time reflecting on each of the three previous points. In addition, it is also important for them to consider how obsessive and compulsive behaviors can be specifically manifested through life experiences, relationships, and, quite often, individual spiritual practices.

With some effort, most scrupulous people can clearly identify moments in their lives in which they have experienced the sacred. Most are also able to recognize how their compulsive and obsessive behaviors, disclosed or not, dramatically influence many of their relationships. Finally, most can acknowledge that there are some specific spiritual practices with which they routinely struggle. In the Roman Catholic tradition, the sacrament of reconciliation and reception of holy Communion come quickly to mind. For Catholics, we acknowledge the importance of participating in the sacraments as a regular and necessary expression of a spiritual life, even when we struggle.

Understanding each of these components is necessary for a fuller appreciation of who we are as spiritual people. However, it is not the complete story. There are three other distinct components that we must also consider and understand: capacity, style/type, and discipline.

Capacity: When Fr. Teilhard de Chardin, SJ, asserted that all human beings are spiritual beings, he emphasized an understanding about the human person that is important for us to realize: all people, because they are human, have an ability and capacity to recognize and engage in at least a basic awareness of and appreciation for the sacred, the mysterious, and the awe-inspiring.

We can understand and appreciate the sacred because we are, to the best of our knowledge, the only creatures on this planet who live in the present, are aware of the past, and enjoy the ability to anticipate the future. In other words, we are not primarily instinctive creatures; we have a level of self-consciousness and the ability to reflect.

A person who has reached a certain level of maturity may determine that he or she will not interpret his or her experience of life (past, present, and future) from a spiritual perspective. Every person has the capacity to make such a decision.

Style/Type: Just as there are many different varieties of flowers in a garden, there are many styles and types of spiritual expression. God seems to be pleased with both the many different flowers and the many different expressions of spiritual awareness. We need not get bogged down by emphasizing different religious expressions, such as Catholic, Evangelical, Jewish, Muslim, or Buddhist. Rather, we can look to the *Catechism* to appreciate this distinctive component of spirituality:

"In many ways, throughout history down to the

PART 1: SPIRITUAL PRACTICES

present day, men have given expression to their quest for God in their religious beliefs and behavior: in their prayers, sacrifices, rituals, meditations, and so forth. These forms of religious expression, despite the ambiguities they often bring with them, are so universal that one may well call man a religious being" (*CCC* 28).

Discipline: An individual must put forth a certain amount of effort to focus his or her spiritual capacity within the specific parameters of a particular style/type of religious expression. Often, attaining a certain expertise or level of comfort requires sustained practice. Human beings know from experience that "practice makes perfect," and, if not perfect, practice at least improves performance in a measurable manner. For example, the first time a person hits a golf ball with a driver, the ball goes only a few feet. However, after disciplined, focused practice sessions, many people can drive the golf ball impressive distances and repeat the feat easily.

Applying these distinct components to the concept of a spiritual life and what it means to be human is hopefully clearer at this point. However, a specific application of these components to the scrupulous person is our goal; otherwise, this would be an incomplete presentation. When we apply each of these realities and components to the experiences of a person who suffers with the religious manifestation of OCD, is there any reality or component that suggests a closer examination to achieve a deeper understanding and clarity? Of course there is, and we will focus on the three components we just reviewed.

While it is possible that a person with scrupulosity might struggle primarily with discipline, most scrupulous people I encounter are very dedicated in their scrupulosity, devoting countless hours a day to it. Looking more closely at style and type of spiritual expression would not provide significant benefit either. Although more Catholics seem to struggle with scrupulosity than do people of other religions, it is not because scrupulosity is a "Catholic" problem. Rather, it is because as Catholics, we have a sacramental system within our style/type of spiritual expression, particularly emphasizing sin and confession, that brings the struggle of scrupulosity into focus more clearly and regularly. That leaves for our consideration only one other component: capacity.

Does a scrupulous person have the capacity to participate in all the specific manifestations of Roman

PART 1: SPIRITUAL PRACTICES

Catholicism in the same manner and with the same expectations as a person without scrupulosity? Does a person with scrupulosity have diminished capacity, through no fault of their own, that makes it difficult, if not impossible, to participate fully in each of the religious disciplines and practices of Roman Catholicism? Do they have a diminished capacity specifically for the sacrament of reconciliation and the spiritual practice of the examination of conscience? If the answer to these questions is "yes," is there any acceptable, orthodox, and morally certifiable choice in which a person might engage so that he or she can live a more integrated and sustainable spirituality? The following example can help us grasp the ramifications of this perspective.

I have often counseled scrupulous men and women about the necessity of checking the publication date when referring to a book that portends to provide pastoral advice. A person without scrupulosity might read a book from the 1800s and profit from some of the discussion therein. For scrupulous men and women, who have a demonstrated inclination to follow directives exactly as they are written, a book from the 1800s may be harmful. The potential harm lies in the fact that nineteenth-century knowledge and understanding of psychology and science are not applicable today. While the advice may have been useful in the 1800s, it is not as useful for people of this age.

I use the power of exaggeration to illustrate my point. If you peruse the owner's manual for a Model T Ford manufactured in the early twentieth century and try to apply the information to a Chevy Malibu from the twenty-first century, you will be forever frustrated. Yes, both are cars, and both are used for transportation. However, the Model T's owner's manual will be severely lacking in any information about the automatic features and computer-driven functions of a modern automobile. Likewise, when an individual is dealing with issues related to mental health and personal well-being, it is best to use the most current advice available. It would be foolhardy not to do so.

Of course, we are speaking about spiritual living and practice, not cars. Some authors of older spiritual books that discuss scrupulosity are canonized saints—men and women of the highest credibility. However, people with scrupulosity experience a diminished capacity to effectively determine which directives or advice may or may not be useful to them. It is because of this diminished capacity—particularly regarding the ability to effectively understand the full consequences of impending decisions—that I consistently counsel scrupulous people to avoid resources that are not up to date.

I do not apply the words "diminished capacity" without serious reflection. It is the direct result of ministering for many years to people who suffer from scrupulosity. I fully understand that scrupulous people often replace their capacity to reasonably accomplish a particular outcome in their spiritual life with heroic acts of discipline and will. In a sense, scrupulous people often try to overcome their lack of capacity to effectively understand the full consequences of their decisions and actions by "toughing it out." This is done in the false belief that it is required by God for the salvation of their souls.

I am convinced that the effects of OCD and the religious manifestation of OCD as scrupulosity contribute to a specific diminished capacity to act in a reasonable and healthy manner in specific instances. One example may be the inability to reasonably benefit from reading a traditional and well-respected book about spirituality. Another example is a struggle with a traditional act of piety and devotion: the examination of conscience.

For a person who does not suffer from scrupulosity,

such an examination provides useful insight and direction. For someone who does suffer from scrupulosity, it often becomes excruciating as he or she painstakingly examines every possible thought and emotion that may be even remotely associated with a particular action. In the latter instance, I assert that a scrupulous person has a diminished capacity to apply the examination of conscience as part of his or her spiritual routine and therefore should not engage in it.

The primary reason that a scrupulous person should avoid an examination of conscience is that, because of the disorder, he or she suffers from the inability to control certain impulses, be they thoughts or actions. When the person engages in the examen and "unleashes" his or her impulse for self-reflection, the results will not be helpful. It is similar to an alcoholic attempting to drink alcohol in moderation. For this person, there is no such thing as a "little bit" or a reasonable amount of alcohol. An alcoholic who desires to be sober must avoid alcohol completely. In the same sense, a scrupulous person who desires to become healthy and live a life free from obsessive and compulsive behavior must avoid at all costs any activity that engages harmful impulses. There are no two ways about it.

PART 1: SPIRITUAL PRACTICES

Most psychologists would agree that to "diagnose" a person with diminished capacity, the degree to which the person has or lacks the capacity to control his or her behavior must be assessed by observing that behavior over time. In other words, this is not a determination that one makes casually; it is serious, because the consequences are most serious. Obviously, this suggests that a regular confessor and/or spiritual director should participate in the process of determining whether specific spiritual practices are useful for individuals suffering from scrupulosity.

For those who like to "read between the lines," the full ramifications of what I am suggesting in this reflection go well beyond simple spiritual reading material and certain acts of piety and devotion. Despite their best effort and the discipline of their will, people who suffer from scrupulosity are unable to find peace and wholeness in their day-to-day living; therefore, certain spiritual practices are most likely out of the question for them. In fact, to actively engage in such practices seriously harms their spiritual lives and well-being, which is the exact opposite of what is intended. In such instances, other avenues of God's grace, perhaps through the sacramental life of the Church, might be more appropriate.

If a person suffers from diminished capacity in the manner I have described, it is a result of OCD. It is most certainly not the result of sin or of a lack of will or effort. It is not an excuse or an attempt to "find the easy way out."

Scrupulous people who desire to integrate their spiritual discipline and practice into a healthy manifestation of God's grace, I encourage you to seek out your confessor and/or spiritual director for a discussion about what you've read here, and it will hopefully lead to a sense of peace in the Lord. For you, this discussion may be the first step in achieving at least the possibility of a truly integrative spirituality that will enhance your experience of life.

PART 1: SPIRITUAL PRACTICES

Abundant Grace

*Hail Mary, full of grace, the Lord is with you;
blessed are you among women, and
blessed is the fruit of your womb, Jesus.*

*Holy Mary, Mother of God, pray for us sinners,
now and at the hour of our death. Amen.*

Recently, I rediscovered an old story that teaches an important truth. According to the story, an old man is sitting at the entrance to a town. Passersby would often ask him questions. One day, a stranger asked him, "What are the people in this town like?"

"What kind of people were in the town that you came from?" asked the old man in reply.

"In the town I just came from," answered the stranger, "the people were kind, generous, and honest. They were wonderful people!"

"You will also find that the people in this town are wonderful," said the old man.

A few hours later, another stranger approached the old man and asked, "What are the people in this town like?"

"What kind of people were in the town that you came from?" asked the old man.

"In the town I just came from," answered the stranger, "the people were cheats and robbers. They were terrible people."

"You will also find that the people in this town are terrible," said the old man.

We see with the eyes of our hearts. If there is love in our heart, we will see love. If there is hatred and hurt in our heart, we will see hatred and hurt. When I am critical of something or someone, even when the criticism is justified, the criticism begins to take on a life of its own. I find that the criticism begins to seep into other parts of my conversations and form my opinions in ways I would not consciously choose. The criticism has become not a judgment of another person but an expression of who I am.

The same is true when I choose to praise something or someone. The praise and the joy I express also begins

PART 1: SPIRITUAL PRACTICES

to take on a life of its own. It seeps into other parts of my conversations and forms my opinions about people and events that I might not consciously choose to make. The joy has become not a judgment of another person but an expression of who I am.

We are often reminded that as members of the body of Christ, we have been challenged by the Lord to be people of peace, joy, hope, and forgiveness. We are to be people who are inspired by the Holy Spirit and molded continuously into witnesses of the kingdom of God. This molding by the Holy Spirit is a powerful activity—the generous gift of sanctifying grace in our lives—but it is also an action that demands our cooperation. Even God, even the power of the Holy Spirit, needs something to work with. We need to cooperate with the grace that has been freely offered to us so we can see and understand in ways that the world might not easily recognize or embrace as essential.

Despite our best intentions, despite all the good we hope for, each of us must honestly acknowledge that sometimes we are not conduits of God's praise and joy. We acknowledge this not to punish ourselves or feel guilty, not to make judgments about or be critical of ourselves, but simply to acknowledge and accept who we are. When acknowledging our decisions or actions that do not build up the body of Christ, we learn to rebound with another action that does build it up.

Recall the friends and disciples of Jesus. When we reflect on their lives, we observe that even they needed to be open to change and improvement. Even the apostles were not always capable of making the best decisions. However, whenever they became aware of mistakes or bad judgment, they were willing to take the necessary steps to repair the damage.

For those who suffer with scrupulosity, a good spiritual practice is committing yourself, in whatever way necessary, to again being open to the Spirit of God working in your life. If you discover you have been critical, judgmental, or harsh in any of your choices or actions, ask the Lord to gently fill you with patience, kindness, and love. Let the peace and joy of Christ reign in your heart and fill you with his life and power.

The place to begin reflection can be within our own hearts, taking the time to examine how we perceive ourselves. I have discovered that many scrupulous people hold harsh judgments and opinions about their own personal shortcomings. Often, they are able to extend compassion and understanding with incredible pa-

PART 1: SPIRITUAL PRACTICES

tience and fortitude toward the people in their lives, but they are reluctant or unable to extend that same compassion and understanding to themselves. Scrupulous people often hold themselves to a higher standard, one that is unattainable and guarantees that they will always come up short.

Beginning today, let us try to be people who extend the mercy, the compassion, and the grace of God into all the crevices of our lives. As we experience the abundant grace of God, we can share that grace with others and be nourished with it in our own lives, confident that we please God and walk with the Spirit of God each day.

The Parable of the Prodigal Son

The Parable of the Lost (Prodigal) Son found in Luke 15:11–32, may be the best known and beloved story that Jesus shared with us. There is probably no parable more commented on or preached about—not only in Christian circles but often in other religious traditions. We usually recognize this powerful drama as the story of the prodigal son or as the story of the forgiving father. Homilies often emphasize the role of either the son or the father, while others concentrate on neither of these but on the reaction of the eldest son. This parable has been studied and analyzed from all possible angles, has been painted by Rembrandt, and has had every possible meaning extracted from it. The only thing that hasn't happened yet is an Andrew Lloyd Webber Broadway musical about it (who knows, he might be working on one!).

And yet,
with all of this,
we still go back to the story,
expecting more,
and seldom being disappointed.

Each of us knows what it is like to be estranged from someone we love. We know the pain, the frustration, the restlessness, the anxiety, the false starts at reconciliation, and the repeating cycle of nursing the wounds, actions, and words that began the situation and continue to fester. Because we know the experience of estrangement and alienation, we are also able to rejoice when the moment of reconciliation comes. We rejoice when the father embraces the son.

However, for all its power and emotion, this moment in the parable—this moment that gives each of us hope—is not a moment of true reconciliation because there was never a real situation of alienation between father and son. The story tells of the younger son's perception that he needs to be reconciled to his father. However, the perception is inaccurate because the father is not alienated. He is constant and persevering in his love. In fact, there has never been—from the father's perspective—a desire for anything more than to have his son home, in his arms and loved unconditionally.

Although there is no need for reconciliation between the father and the younger son, there still remains a need for reconciliation in the parable. There is a mutual estrangement between the two brothers that needs to be resolved. As the parable ends, we are unsure, although hopeful, that their relationship will be healed.

For our purposes, the relationship between the father and the son is paramount, especially the notion of perceived estrangement. A perception is an assumption that something exists or that a situation is in effect because of the way a person feels or because of the judgments a person makes. Such feelings and judgments feed into the person's belief system, and he or she acts accordingly. It is easy for assumptions and judgments to skew the truth and reality of a situation.

In the parable, the younger son perceives that his actions—taking his father's money, living with reckless abandon, coming to a point of total and irreversible loss—mean that he "no longer deserve[s] to be called [his father's] son" (Luke 15:21). Because of his guilt, the son assumes his father feels the same way. His father does not.

The father does not consider his son's bad choices and unfortunate actions as having anything to do with their relationship. In short, the father refuses to confirm the son's assumptions about himself and his relationship with his father. The father's reaction demonstrates some very appealing qualities—unconditional love, perseverance and faith in relationships, an openness to change of circumstance, the ability to see the "big picture."

PART 1: SPIRITUAL PRACTICES

It is good that our God refuses to confirm the judgments and assumptions we make about ourselves and our relationship with him. "Nor are your ways my ways" (Isaiah 55:8). God our Father does not see or judge the way we do. This is the Good News of the Gospel, the Good News of the kingdom of God. Even when we are not able to see the possibilities or recognize that we are loved, our inability does not change the reality that we are loved, accepted, and forgiven. For scrupulous people, this should provide abundant hope. We should never tire of giving God thanks and praise for this reality and for his gift of abundant grace.

How often do we perceive that we are somehow estranged from God? How often do we perceive that our sins are so bad and our guilt so incomprehensible that God can no longer love us? Yet, despite our perceptions, despite the depth of our feelings and condition, God will not and does not confirm them. Like the example of the father and the son in the parable, God our Father will not confirm our assumptions about him. God desires to be with us forever. God desires that we experience his unconditional love for us. God perseveres in his love for us, despite our lack of commitment. God desires that his relationship with us endures forever.

A good practice is to reflect often on the distorting power of inaccurate or unsubstantiated perceptions as well as to reflect often on the overwhelming evidence presented in the Scriptures that God calls each of us to himself. We are loved and precious in his eyes, and God desires to be with us for all of eternity. Contrast this with your feelings, which may distort your perception of the truth and attempt to take away what God desires for you.

Are you the only exception? The only person who is not and cannot be loved by God? Are you the only person that God ignores and desires to punish for all eternity? No! That is not who God is. That is not the Father that Jesus presents to us in the powerful story of the prodigal son and the forgiving father.

A Fondness for Excess

In *The Parables of Jesus: A Commentary,* author Arland J. Hultgren writes, "The Kingdom of God as proposed by Jesus creates a 'fondness for excess,' a sense of God that is able to interrupt and confound, contradict and confront the established order of things."

These are words I find deeply challenging and, at the

PART 1: SPIRITUAL PRACTICES

same time, comforting. They cause me to pause and reflect. The concept that Jesus seemingly preferred "excess" is one to ponder.

My own reflection of this passage has helped me to probe and accept the foundational charism of the Redemptorist Congregation founded by St. Alphonsus Liguori. Saint Alphonsus believed in "plentiful redemption for all" in the abundance of God's grace, manifested in the people, events, and experiences of our world. Again, I have both wrestled with this concept and found these words comforting, primarily because they help me understand that the manifestation of God's grace is the work, the activity of God, and that this manifestation of grace is not dependent on my poor and incomplete efforts; it is God's gift to his people. Most of us spend a lifetime growing to accept and practice this perspective and truth.

If you struggle to live daily as a person who believes in this powerful manifestation of God's grace, you may appreciate some insights. Once such insight, gleaned from what I have learned during my life, is to adopt a particular spiritual practice, which I will explain further. This practice provides a way (by no means the only way) to enable the lesson of God's "plentiful redemption" to take deeper root in your heart and soul. The practice I incorporate into my daily spiritual life is a type of examen encouraged by St. Alphonsus.

This examen is not an examination of conscience, searching high and low for the manifestation of sin in your life. Rather, using the same devoted energy you would for an examination of conscience, you reflect daily not only on sin but also on the power of God's grace at work in your life. In my spiritual practice of this particular examen, I pay close attention to the language I use to describe my daily living and perceptions about life.

I find it especially important in my examen to pay attention to two distinct concepts: the concept of scarcity and the concept of abundance. The words I choose to describe my experience of life that limit God's grace are illustrative of scarcity. The words I choose to describe my experience of life that allow room for God's grace to be powerfully manifested are illustrative of abundance.

To explain further, when I am operating from a perception that sees life primarily through the lens of scarcity, I use corresponding language. The language of scarcity is based on conditions, "shoulds," fears, anxieties, doubts, and the like. At its root, this belief states

PART 1: SPIRITUAL PRACTICES

that everything needs to be protected, measured, and parceled out so you will not run out. It is a language that will not give an inch, will never presume innocence, demands justice, is never satisfied or completed, and does not believe in forgiveness—"How often must I forgive [my brother]? As many as seven times?" (Matthew 18:21). It is a way of life based on the conviction that there is never enough, and what little you do have might not be sufficient.

When I am operating from a perception that sees life primarily through the lens of abundance, I also use corresponding language. The language of abundance is grounded in the belief that God is filled with plenty. At its core, this belief states that love gives life, that all will be accomplished and fulfilled according to the plan of God, and that forgiveness generates hope—"not seven times but seventy-seven times" (Matthew 18:22). It is the experience of invitation, encouragement, confidence, gratefulness, and generosity.

In comparing these two perceptions, your reflection will lead you further away from asking yourself *What I am doing?* and closer to *How can I enable what I believe to become part of my lived experience?* There is a difference between the "what" and the "how." You can be an expert on what is required in life, but that knowledge will be useless unless you learn how to use it by practicing it and living it out daily.

The aforementioned author, who challenges us to see Jesus as someone who is fond of the excesses of God's life and love, understands this fundamental difference, as did Jesus. Jesus recognized that the scribes and Pharisees were experts in the law but did not actually permit it to animate and energize their lives. As a result, their faith seemed dull and uninspiring. On the other hand, Jesus recognized the efforts of those who, though far from the perfection required by the law, tried to live out the values of the law. They often came up short, yet they had moments in their lives when they were captured by the grace of God and became instruments of the kingdom of God.

This type of daily examen may be beneficial in your own spiritual life and practice. Just make sure that it is about gratefulness and recognizing God's blessings in your life. If it is all about sin, it will not be helpful at all. It may help those with scrupulosity to take the focus off the "what," which is all-consuming, and begin to emphasize the "how," which is full of life and grace.

PART 1: SPIRITUAL PRACTICES

The Unreflective Life

I came across the following story in a collection of old homilies I preached, and its lesson continues to be relevant.

It was market day in the city of Athens. Everyone was trying to find a bargain, and they were not averse to using their tongues and elbows to aid them in the task. In one corner of the market, however, there was a strange quiet: someone whom most people admired and respected walked among the crowd. He was a famous man who had condescended to patronize the marketplace. People moved aside to let him walk by. He wasn't a film or television star, nor was he a member of the royal household—it was still BC. He was an orator, renowned for his eloquence and patronage of lost causes.

There was something very odd about his appearance. Despite being a rich man, he wore tattered clothes; he dressed in rags with the diligence and care others took with formal clothing. He was clearly pleased at the theatrical impression he was making on the onlookers, until a voice in the crowd hailed him: "Antisthenes, Antisthenes, I can see your pride through the hole in your cloak." For once, the great orator had nothing to say.

According to the story, Antisthenes had nothing to say because he was trying to pass himself off as someone he was not. He was guilty of trying to deceive others into thinking well of him and embracing a false projection of him. It was a shallow attempt to divert attention away from his true self, and it reduced the great orator to silence when the farce was discovered.

The story reminds me of the consistent teaching of Jesus and his invitation to conversion and new life. Time and again, Jesus takes to task people who are willing to notice faults in others but are blind to their own shortcomings, thereby portraying themselves as people they clearly are not. It is important to understand what Jesus is confronting when he brings a person face to face with this behavior. The sin is not in recognizing faults in another person but rather in one's failure to recognize and accept his or her personal faults and weaknesses. The sin is in pretending to be someone he or she is not.

The worst part of this behavior is the clear warning

PART 1: SPIRITUAL PRACTICES

sign of an "unreflective life." As the Apostle James says, "For if anyone is a hearer of the word and not a doer, he is like a man who looks at his own face in a mirror. He sees himself, then goes off and promptly forgets what he looked like" (James 1:23–24). The unreflective life is unaware of what truth is. It is a life convinced that others can be just as easily fooled as you are. It is a life in which you repeat the thoughts and opinions of others because you are completely unaware of your own thoughts and feelings.

In an unreflective life, you never discover the truth about yourself; you never honestly enter a relationship because you do not know who you are. It is a life in which you are doomed to keep pretending.

People who are unreflective, who do not know the truth about themselves, are threatened by the faults and failings of others. They live their lives like they are in a dream. Unaware of who they are, they move through life feeling threatened by anyone and anything that might expose their true personalities.

You can imitate various qualities, such as being talented, funny, or loyal, but if you do not truly know who you are and why you are loved by God, then, at best, you are an actor. There is a big difference between living the life you are called to through baptism and being an actor. One is real, and the other is a flattering imitation.

The spiritual life demands honesty, integrity, the willingness to recognize yourself as both saint and sinner, and the willingness to celebrate who you are. The spiritual life invites others to wholeness and healthiness but does not need to demand, insist, or threaten. Finally, the spiritual life accepts others exactly as they are because you see that all people are redeemed and called into the fullness of life.

Scrupulosity can make people truly unaware of who they are. When we look at only a portion of ourselves, focusing all our energy and anxiety on certain sins or behaviors, we are incomplete. When we resist God's call to step back and look beyond our biggest fears and anxieties to see something more, we risk living unreflective lives. When we can easily list all our faults and failings—behaviors and shortcomings we name as sin—but cannot list our gifts and talents, something significant is missing from our lives. We are just like Antisthenes, walking through the marketplace and completely unaware that our true selves are on display for all to see.

One of the tendencies of scrupulosity is to quickly notice and identify the faults of others. Because people

PART 1: SPIRITUAL PRACTICES

with scrupulosity struggle so valiantly with the fears and anxieties of their own shortcomings, they are more prone to seeing the same in others. That being the case, a life of grace is also present in each person—in our individual selves and in the people on whom we focus our particular concerns. If we want to be authentic, aware, and open to all the gifts and graces that come from God, we must also try to recognize and accept all aspects of who we are, not just pieces.

PART 2

CRITICAL BELIEFS

The scrupulous condition is a terrible affliction. The constant questions, anxiety, and doubts are everyday experiences that seem never-ending; additionally, certain empathetic beliefs are a shared experience within the scrupulous community. I identify these beliefs as empathetic because, when they are expressed, it is impossible not to hear and feel the emotion and depth of conviction present in the scrupulous person. When such a belief finally finds an outlet and is either discussed in private conversation with a confessor, shared with a trusted friend, or expressed in another manner, the scrupulous person experiences a sense of relief, along with real pain and suffering.

Over the years, I have attempted to identify some of these beliefs and reflect on the accompanying emotions. I do not pretend to have understood the true depth of the experience or exhausted the full range of emotions, but I believe I have captured some common beliefs and emotions that may be useful to analyze. This section of the book provides a good start but is not a complete presentation.

Each of the reflections that follow are intended to provide encouragement to the person who suffers with and experiences these beliefs and emotions. It is my hope that each reflection will help you enter your spiritual practice a little less burdened. I also hope the context provided will help you accept what you are experiencing, hopefully reducing your anxiety and feelings of helplessness.

Each reflection may be useful to incorporate as an occasional spiritual practice, especially on those occasions when you are experiencing strong emotions or compulsions to lose hope against the daily struggle with scrupulosity. It can be very reassuring to know that, despite the strong feelings, the power of grace is all the more present and active.

PART 2: CRITICAL BELIEFS

I am helpless, caught in a never-ending spiral of emotion, guilt, and anxiety.

Realtors often say that one of the most essential components of a valuable property is "location, location, location." No matter if you are considering a property for a home or a business, the location is essential. Location determines the price you will pay, and it often also determines how much the property value will grow or decrease over the years.

Likewise, for a person with scrupulosity, an essential perception is "context, context, context." Context makes all the difference in regard to the questions or subject matter under discussion. If a person can resist the temptation to ask narrowly focused questions that eliminate the true contextual nature of the questions, then there is a better chance of arriving at helpful, informed answers. If, on the other hand, the context is minimized or eliminated, the answer is potentially skewed and perhaps even harmful. The scrupulous person's compulsion to minimize, however, is very strong and compelling.

To understand this, it may be helpful to think of a whirlpool that naturally forms in a stream or lake. At the bottom of the whirlpool is an intense energy that whirls in ever tighter circles, spinning much faster than the water at the top. It seems that the energy at the bottom of the whirlpool is much more intense than that at the top. However, the same amount of energy is used from top to bottom; it is just an illusion that more energy is being expended when the water spins in tighter circles.

I imagine the person caught in the obsessive-compulsive whirlpool of scrupulosity is experiencing the frantic energy at the bottom of the spiral. A person who is not in this obsessive-compulsive spiral is operating from a much larger base—a context that enables him or her to see and experience the "bigger picture." It is the same experience and consumption of energy but an entirely different focus and result when applied to a specific question, fear, or anxiety.

For some reason, obsessive and compulsive behaviors channel energy into tighter, more restrictive "spirals." The person is slowly drawn into a spiral that eliminates the larger context and instead focuses his or her attention on the smallest possible component. In the process, the person becomes convinced, because of what he or she is experiencing, that this smallest component is what is most important. A single, small part that is out

PART 2: CRITICAL BELIEFS

of place or imperfect destroys and effectively changes the larger experience for the person, making it severely and permanently flawed. If the component is a question, a moral issue, or a challenge, it has the potential to lead a person into mortal sin, which is the most permanent and damaging judgment possible: condemnation for all eternity. Of course, the possibility of mortal sin is not really in question; the fear of possibly sinning is what is paramount at this point.

The smaller and more focused the question, anxiety, or fear providing the impetus for the frantic energy, the more certain it is that the context has become minimized. Instead of understanding the struggle within a larger context, which may explain some of the emotion, any possibility of another interpretation or understanding is eliminated, and all that remains is the feeling of spiraling out of control.

I arrived at this conclusion when listening to participants at a retreat describe their experiences of scrupulosity. They were experiencing what it means to be human in a tightly constricted "whirlpool of energy." They found themselves, despite their best efforts, being dragged deeper into the spiral of despair. Some were convinced there was no way out of the spiral, while others held out for some hope or miracle that would release them from the torment, fear, and anxiety.

I understood clearly for the first time that there was no way I could offer anything to potentially free them from this experience. All my answers, advice, and encouragement mean absolutely nothing to a person in the grips of this type of experience. I also realized that these people were not expecting me to heal or free them. While they appreciated that I was struggling to understand their experience, they desired something well beyond my feeble efforts. They desired to be reassured that they were loved and accepted by God, despite their pain and suffering.

The people who shared their stories of being trapped in the spiral of OCD and scrupulosity wanted to be assured that God was not inflicting this upon them. They needed to be assured that they had not been singled out for torment or punishment. Rather, scrupulosity is a cruel juxtaposition of pathology, biology, and psychology, no different than any other illness or disease experienced by men and women each day. It has nothing to do with people's inherent "goodness," and it most certainly is not a predictor of their experience of eternal life or worthiness for salvation.

PART 2: CRITICAL BELIEFS

During the retreat, I assured the participants individually that they were loved and accepted by God, exactly as they were, not as they one day might be. At the same time, I did not abandon the hope and power of grace, and I tried to lead them to a place where they felt free enough to risk perceiving their lives and religious experiences in a different way. I advised them that "widen the picture" and "change the context" are mantras that offer some hope of healing, some concrete manifestation of God's grace at work. I urged them to try to resist the ritual that sets off the spiral and reminded them that it is worth the effort to resist and learn behavioral skills that will help them in the process. With this advice and encouragement, more than one person expressed newfound confidence to try or to redouble their efforts. Unfortunately, but very understandably, others were too discouraged or exhausted by the constant effort and were fearful that any more effort on their part was useless.

Despite the persistent power of the OCD spiral to draw each scrupulous person more deeply into minute detail, along with fear and anxiety, the power of God's grace is not ineffective. The scrupulous person's powerful feelings of hopelessness do not signal defeat or uselessness. Yes, the struggle is intense and at times overwhelming, but the grace of God will prevail. Nothing can change the ultimate destiny of God's people, which is manifested by the power of the Spirit of God.

PART 2: CRITICAL BELIEFS

I am taking advantage of God's love and mercy for me.

I received the following letter from a regular listener to my radio program, and I think it is quite poignant and sincere. I originally intended to answer it in the *Scrupulous Anonymous* newsletter, but, upon further reflection, I decided that it warranted a detailed response. The letter captures a feeling that is often experienced by people who suffer with scrupulosity but is not often presented as clearly.

Dear Father,

I think I have been suffering from scrupulosity for a year or two now. Confession for me is difficult because I feel like I often confess things that are not really sins, but I am not sure. When I do an examination of conscience, I feel that sometimes I cannot think of my sins regarding a commandment, yet I know I am sinning all the time. I just found your website and recognize myself in some of the "Ten Commandments for the Scrupulous."

Anyway, I do my best and try to confess sins I really have committed, but here is my problem.

When I think of letting go of my sense of remorse and guilt over my former very bad and sinful behavior when I was young (sins of debauchery that I have done my best to confess fully), I feel like, if I do, I am cheapening what it cost our Lord for what I've done. In other words, to let myself be happy again feels like I am not grateful—like someone paid a million-dollar fine for me, and I said a quick "thanks a lot" and went on my merry way (being happy again). How can I let go of my remorse and guilt without getting a sense that I am treating God like a chump?

God is not a chump! A chump is a person who is foolish or easily deceived. By any stretch of the imagination, it would be quite difficult to identify our Father in heaven in this manner. The Father is intimately aware of each person, including not only our weaknesses but also our strengths. Our innermost thoughts, desires, and attitudes are completely and totally revealed to our heavenly Father. He knows and understands us completely, and because he knows us better than we know ourselves, he is neither foolish nor easily deceived.

A better way of stating this feeling is to put the emphasis on ourselves and not on God. What the writer is really trying to describe is that it is incomprehensible to him that God is completely willing to love and forgive him. The truth is that God's all-encompassing and redeeming love is unlimited and always offered freely and completely to all his creation, in all places, and despite potentially compromising circumstances and events. Remember that God's love for you cannot be compromised; it is an eternal love. You might not understand or appreciate the full extent of this reality, but it nevertheless describes your relationship with God. It is not dependent on you; it is an unmerited gift from God.

You are most certainly not alone in your inability to fully accept or comprehend this kind of love. Generally, human beings are not capable of loving in this manner. The love that we offer another person or that we experience ourselves is often conditional love. Despite our best intentions and efforts, that seems to always be the case. Perhaps the reason we routinely experience conditional love is because we are not capable of fully experiencing the building blocks of love that are the foundation for authentic relationships: truth, vulnerability, and intimacy.

To know, understand, and accept who you are as a

person means that you must be willing to see yourself exactly as you are, not as you one day might be. To experience this truth, you must acknowledge that you are very much a "work in progress," constantly growing and developing. At the same time, you also possess a specific past, present, and future.

Each of us is a creation limited by our experience. Our concept of God, however, goes beyond limits and boundaries. Because God is the Creator of time past, time present, and time future, he is not limited in any manner. This limitlessness means that God is the ultimate reality and ultimate truth. There is nothing that needs to be shaped, molded, or improved. God is totally and completely complete.

God, who is Creator and all powerful, has freely chosen to be exposed to an unnecessary vulnerability. God has chosen to offer his love to his creation—us—and he permits us to freely return or withhold that love. God invites and enables love but does not demand it as a condition for life. Our lives are not immediately snuffed out if we refuse to return his love for us.

God's vulnerability enables his love for his creatures to be more creative and vibrant because it is offered freely. It is the ultimate risk of relationship but is nevertheless a choice God enables us to make. When we freely chose to return God's love to him, the Father rejoices; when we choose to not return his love, God still continues to love us. God never rejects his freely assumed vulnerability but goes so far as to permit his creatures to live with a false sense of freedom, pretending they are in charge and in control. All the while, God waits patiently for each person to experience an awakening that will invite the person back into the authentic dynamic of relationship.

This dynamic and experience speak to us of a wonderful, but at the same time incomprehensible, mystery. It shows us an intimacy in relationships we often believe is not possible because it is so far outside our own experience. However, when we hear the description of this kind of relationship, our hearts leap with joy and expectation. Can this be true? Can there be a love that is unconditional and that I can claim for myself?

The answer is a resounding yes! Yet it is also the incomprehensible part of the experience mentioned by the letter writer. It is perhaps the primary reason we hold on to remorse and guilt instead of rejoicing over the gift of grace we have received. By clinging to something that makes us feel incomplete and undeserving, we are trying to maintain an illusion of control. God does not want us to live with illusions but to live and celebrate our lives in freedom as his children.

God is no chump. The mystery of God's grace and God's life at work in our lives is a pure gift to each of us. Let go of the remorse, let go of the guilt, and try to live in the freedom that only God can give to his creation.

Scrupulosity is demanding. There are so many rules and rituals that must be followed perfectly.

When reading the New Testament, we routinely encounter one of the groups of people that seemed to be a favorite focus of Jesus' teaching. The Pharisees were one of the religious groups within Israel who influenced the daily lives of the people of the time. Every facet of life was regulated, influenced, and, in a very real sense, controlled by the Pharisees' interpretation of what was required to be a religious person. Perhaps this is one reason that the Pharisees come so clearly into focus when we encounter Jesus in the Scriptures.

During the time of Jesus, there were more than 600 specific commandments that needed to be obeyed to live a life that, according to the Pharisees, was pleasing to God. Some of these commandments were undoubtedly very useful; Jesus left them intact and unchallenged. Yet other commandments were the specific focus of his teaching and occasionally of his frustration and, sometimes, anger.

The big picture that emerges from the teaching of Jesus is the general pronouncement that the teachers of the law, including the Pharisees, had placed too many burdens and expectations on the people. Jesus offers a different way—a new way of living that gives praise and glory to God. "Come to me.... For my yoke is easy, and my burden light" (Matthew 11:28–30). The message of Jesus presents an invitation to a life that today we understand is the life of the kingdom of God.

Notice, however, in the invitation, there is an expectation, an essential first step. The expectation is to be familiar with what was once required and then to become aware of what is now possible. It is most certainly not an invitation to a life in which there are no expectations, rules, or requirements. Rather, Jesus invites you to something more, not less.

The person who accepts the yoke of Jesus accepts a new way of living, a new perspective that ultimately leads to freedom and the fullness of life. Today, we understand that this way of living leads to life everlasting. Yes, it still presents challenges and struggles, but the burden and yoke are necessary parts of Jesus' invitation to a new way of life, and they are easy and light when we enter into relationship with him.

Saint Alphonsus Liguori teaches that if people love God, those people can do what they please. At first glance, this sounds carte blanche, but it is not. Saint Alphonsus understood that for people to enter into relationship with the Lord, they must become aware of the presence of God at work in their lives. Only then does a fundamental change occur within. A relationship with God will so fill, change, and capture a person that it is impossible to choose, do, or hope for anything that does not give glory and honor to God. This does not eliminate the possibility of weakness, failure, and sin but instead places each of these realities of our human existence within a larger context as part of human living that ultimately pleases God. In Jesus' time, this was a profound and revolutionary spiritual insight, and it remains so for us today.

Not unlike the Pharisees, people today can quite easily get caught up in the details of life. It is tempting to take refuge in learning and obeying all the rules and the regulations, down to the most minute points, somehow being assured that this is God's will for his people. We might even fall into the temptation, and often the sin, of insisting that this is the only way to live, to perceive reality, and give glory to God.

Jesus calls all of us to something more. He calls us to see life in a way that celebrates the presence of God not only in the details but also in the people, events, and circumstances that are part of God's creation. If we can learn to see as Jesus sees, if we can learn to perceive life in the kingdom of God, then we will truly understand what it means to experience both the yoke and the burden of the Lord—and it will free us, not weigh us down. Our hearts and spirits will soar, and we will be able to believe and participate with confidence in all the Lord has gifted us with each day.

For people who struggle with the burden of scrupulosity, this is particularly difficult. The details seem so important and necessary, and while they are, we should not become so consumed by them that they deprive us of peace. We need balance, and therein lies the real challenge.

PART 2: CRITICAL BELIEFS

I am the only person who understands my experience of scrupulosity.

Recently, I spoke with a priest about scrupulosity, and he asked me this question: "What is the most difficult component or manifestation of scrupulosity for people who do not have the affliction to understand?"

Any number of possible appropriate responses immediately came to mind. I could have replied that it is the intensity of the never-ending questioning and the anxiety it fuels. I could have offered the observation that many priests, trained in the classic moral understanding of scrupulosity, believe they are dealing with "tender conscience" and, as a result, routinely misdiagnose the condition and thus do not offer the appropriate pastoral response. I also could have talked about scrupulosity as a specific and focused manifestation of OCD. Each of these answers would have been insightful and valuable.

However, I chose a distinctly different response: "The most difficult component is that each scrupulous person experiences his or her own manifestation of scrupulosity, and that person is the only one who knows and understands all the rules."

In other words, each person with scrupulosity suffers with his or her own "brand" of the disorder. Scrupulous people certainly share specific components—fear, anxiety, constant questioning, specific rituals—but each manifestation is complex and unique to the individual. When dealing with scrupulosity, there is no such thing as "one size fits all." It has taken me a long time to understand this reality and adjust my own thinking.

Early in my ministry with the scrupulous, I often thought that part of the scrupulous dynamic was that, somewhere along the line, as the affliction progressed, each person would begin to define his or her own "brand." I would flippantly describe scrupulosity as "terminal uniqueness," which, although it sounds harsh and judgmental, is unfortunately very insightful.

When a person is constantly bombarded with questions and doubt fueled by never-ending anxiety and fear, there is no way he or she can manage any kind of sustainable life or relationships. The first step in defining the "brand" of scrupulosity is to define when and where it is operative, and when and where it is not. For example, someone who is paralyzed when confronted with a moral decision will routinely make other types of decisions each day. The person's scrupulosity is not focused on decision-making in general; it is rather narrowly focused on the singular issue of morality.

Another person with the OCD manifestation of scrupulosity may be free of anxiety and guilt about routine moral decisions but experiences paralyzing fear when faced with decisions about relationships. Still others may worry about sexuality, or finances, or something else, all the while never experiencing the same type of worry in other areas of their lives.

The first step in branding an individual's scrupulosity always necessitates defining the boundaries and the subject matter. Of course, a person is not presented with a menu of choices to pick and choose from. Defining boundaries results from scrupulosity's inability to be omnipresent in all shapes and forms at any time.

What this means is that there are many times in a day when a person with scrupulosity does not engage in his or her obsession(s) and compulsion(s). If the person understood this reality and made the connection that he or she experiences some freedom each day, he or she could make some real progress toward true healing.

Unfortunately, this does not happen, because the person's unique brand of scrupulosity becomes operative. When the person then spends time unraveling the main source of scrupulosity, he or she discovers that it is even more refined and focused than imagined. For example, the person does not struggle with the general area of morality but rather parses it to the point where only certain questions and dilemmas provoke fear and anxiety. These narrowly focused areas of concern are further delineated into the smallest components, each of which can ignite the OCD ritual and fuel an emotional response.

This strategy—gradually identifying the primary area of concern and its specific components—sounds like potential progress and healing but is in fact a dead end. As soon as a person begins to exhaust the potential questions and doubts about a particular issue, he or she will abandon that issue and replace it with a new concern. The new concern will be very closely related to the original, just different enough to provide a new and untested series of questions.

This is where the despair and helplessness often experienced by scrupulous people ultimately take its toll: as soon as they experience some sense of progress, hope, and a manifestation of grace, the subject matter shifts. It is as if they sense relief is on the horizon and unconsciously make the necessary adjustments to maintain their scrupulosity at the level with which they are familiar. They seem to claim their individual brands of scrupulosity and seize their unique experiences, perhaps fearing what will happen next if the familiar but unwelcome "houseguest" departs.

When scrupulous people spend enormous amounts of energy maintaining their primary areas of concern, mainly through unsuccessful rituals that falsely promise relief, scrupulosity is victorious. When they devote excruciating care and concern to maintaining their particular brands of scrupulosity, the affliction is dominant. Are we referring to sin, moral guilt, or responsibility in this matter? Absolutely not! What we are speaking about is a pathological affliction—an illness that wreaks havoc and routinely deprives people of joy and peace in their lives.

In and of itself, this insight has solved nothing but is still valuable. The more we discover about the manifestation of scrupulosity, both in general and regarding your particular brand, the more we take small steps toward a day where you can learn to manage, if not cure, this terrible affliction. This is something we all hope and pray for daily.

Mortal sin is like the bogeyman, waiting for me around every corner.

When I listen to people with scrupulosity talk about sin, especially about mortal sin, I experience an uncomfortable feeling. Scrupulous people imagine mortal sin as some sort of character, a personification. They perceive mortal sin as something like the mythical bogeyman, lurking around every corner, waiting to pounce and snare them into a state of serious sinfulness. In this unfortunate scenario, every thought, word, or action, no matter how seemingly innocent or normal, is a potential hiding place for this personification of the affliction. As a result of this perception and the fear it generates, scrupulous people assume they must always take the utmost care and caution in all circumstances, lest they unwittingly fall into the trap. With this kind of diligence and focus, there is often little room for any sense of peace, fulfillment, or happiness.

Unlike the bogeyman, who is a mythical character at best, the fear and anxiety generated by this personification of mortal sin is palatable. I have experienced the painful manifestation of this emotion in people firsthand in a variety of settings. For them, it is more than

PART 2: CRITICAL BELIEFS

an allusion and is perceived as real because it fills them with anxiety and fear. However, no matter the feeling or how convinced they might be that the personification of mortal sin is capable of sending them with a one-way ticket to hell, nothing could be further from the truth.

Mortal sin is not a person, a devil, or any other personification. Mortal sin is not lurking behind every bush or in every nook and cranny. Mortal sin is a descriptive and theological understanding that is useful for the formation of the conscience. Whenever a person feels something, including very strong emotions, it is not a signal that the bogeyman has appeared. It is also not a signal to the conscience that a mortal sin is imminent.

There are a variety of human experiences intended to be enjoyed and engaged in with an intensity of emotion that is not sinful. This range of human emotion includes such things as the expression of justified anger, the feeling of loss and disappointment that leads to tears, and the physical experience of sexuality. Any of these can cause a strong manifestation of emotions to surge through a person, whether deliberately engaged in or as a secondary experience. None of these are necessarily experiences of sin, despite the intensity of emotion.

The list of strong and intense human experiences is almost endless. In each instance, these experiences are not the least bit sinful. Many times, the resultant feelings are the intended and most appropriate expression. To say otherwise is to contradict and ultimately hold in disrespect the act of Creation as it is intended by the Creator God.

Human decisions and experiences are not intended to be constantly categorized into good or bad, sinful or not sinful, mortal or venial. Life is not a test filled with traps, mazes, and other illusions intended to obscure the face of God for the person who seeks a relationship with him. The teachings and the spirit of the Second Vatican Council invite the people of God to change their perspectives and viewpoints to perceive a completely different dynamic and relationship.

If you remain unconvinced by the teaching of the Council, you can go to the original source for inspiration and clarification. The word of God as it has been preserved for us in the sacred Scriptures invites us to widen our perception and change our attitudes. I can state this with the clearest sense of conviction and offer the words of Jesus that are applicable: "If you then, who are wicked, know how to give good gifts to your children, how much more will the Father in heaven give the Holy Spirit to those who ask him?" (Luke 11:13).

In analyzing this passage, it is fair to ask these questions: What cruel parent would dangle their love and affection in front of their son or daughter and then snatch it away at the last moment? What kind of cruel parent would set their son or daughter on a path with the promise that it will lead to something important, and then fill that path with obstacles that make the journey impossible? What parent would give difficult instructions for the journey to one child, and then provide their other children with an unobstructed path to the destination? Scrupulous people often perceive others this way—everyone walks on the same path, but others seem to do so with little or no difficulty, certainly free of anxiety and guilt over the smallest things.

I understand there is a sense of comfort in the idea of personifying moral decisions. Such a personification makes decision-making something "out there affecting me" rather than something "within me as a human person." The way to freedom is not to view life and its experiences as something that happens to you, but rather as something that you fully, to the best of your ability, participate in. There is no bogeyman intent on trapping or confusing you. Our God is a God of relationship who desires to be with us on the journey. That is the Good News of the kingdom of God.

PART 2: CRITICAL BELIEFS

Priests do not understand me.

Once, after I returned from conducting a scrupulous retreat, one of my confreres asked, "Did anyone actually attend the retreat?" I replied that the retreat had been well attended by a diverse group of people, all different ages and professions. The diversity was not unexpected and was reflective of those who understood they needed help, regardless of what else was going on in their lives. Despite their differences, what each person had in common was that they suffered from a specific manifestation of OCD in matters of religious practice, specifically Roman Catholicism. My confrere expressed surprise and reacted with a somewhat dismissive response: "I thought all of that would be over at this point in our development as a Church."

This confrere, a very wise and holy priest, was laboring under a common misconception about scrupulosity. He understood scrupulosity in the traditional way, primarily as the manifestation of a "tender conscience." What he did not know is that there is another, more serious, manifestation of scrupulosity for some individuals. For these people, there are no quick fixes, regardless of how patient or understanding their confessors may be.

People who suffer not from a tender conscience but from OCD are afflicted for a prolonged period with a psychological imbalance. They suffer from a diminished capacity to make effective and helpful decisions and moral judgments about their spiritual lives. This diminished capacity does not result from a lack of catechetical training, nor is it descriptive of a state of sinfulness. It is a painful and unrelenting torment that strikes at the very heart of what these people hold most dear: their understanding, experience, and practice of spirituality and their relationship with God.

My confrere's misunderstanding of the scrupulous condition was discussed during the scrupulous retreat: "Why is it that so many priests do not understand what I am going through?" "Why is there no help or guidance when I need it the most?" This frustration is shared by many.

I offer a partial answer that may be helpful to some. It is true that many priests do not seem to know about or understand the scrupulous condition except for the minimal training they received in seminary, which likely considered scrupulosity as a manifestation of a tender conscience. It would be rare for a seminary to spend sufficient time speaking about the manifestation

PART 2: CRITICAL BELIEFS

of OCD within the context of religious obsessions or compulsions.

Why is this training beyond the realm of reasonable expectation? The answer is found in the reality of the situation. The men and women who suffer from this manifestation represent a very small number of people who consider themselves Catholic and an even smaller number of people who regularly incorporate the sacrament of reconciliation into their spiritual practice. Seminary training, by necessity, concentrates on the development of skills that are necessary for ordinary pastoral care, not necessarily extraordinary pastoral care.

Although the number of people who suffer from scrupulosity is small compared to the entire Roman Catholic population, their suffering is intense and acute because they often suffer quietly. They frequently believe they are alone and not cared for. They seldom share their true condition and experiences of anguish unless they and their struggles are masked in anonymity by a confessional wall. Their suffering may not appear regularly on the "ordinary pastoral care radar," but, for the scrupulous, it is a daily occurrence.

From my limited perspective, I do not foresee a

change in seminary pastoral training, but I sense that perhaps, as in many other pastoral encounters, we might hope for a growing awareness among priests so that they understand what they are encountering when they come face-to-face with scrupulosity. I hope we can arrive at a point where most confessors can at least offer the scrupulous helpful referrals to professionals trained in the necessary guidance and support. Encouragement from a confessor to seek professional help and guidance would be very helpful for those with scrupulosity; I cannot stress how beneficial this would be.

Until there is a change in pastoral practice, the best we can hope for is the traditional response, where the scrupulous person has a patient, kindly, and supportive confessor. It's also beneficial for priests to share the resources they use with the scrupulous. Priests often seek advice and encouragement from other priests, and the more aware they are of the real suffering of OCD in the religious manifestation of scrupulosity, the better off everyone will be.

PART 2: CRITICAL BELIEFS

Only people with scrupulosity experience unwanted thoughts and feelings; everyone else is normal.

For me, one of the privileges of working with men and women who suffer from scrupulosity is that I am often engaged in personal dialogue with many of you. I can listen to your stories and concerns. I find people who suffer with this affliction to be some of the kindest and most gentle people I have ever met. This critical belief is also an observation about the ravages of scrupulosity; it so often afflicts people who are sensitive and caring, people who believe in their relationship with God and deeply desire to be faithful in that relationship.

Another observation I have made is one that seems to be a favorite fantasy of the scrupulous community: people who do not suffer from scrupulosity never experience powerful unwanted thoughts or feelings. This misconception presumes that people without scrupulosity somehow move through life in complete and total control of their thoughts and emotions, never experiencing a single unexpected moment. Nothing could be further from the truth, no matter how deeply rooted this fantasy is among the scrupulous.

All people, including the great saints of the Church, experience unwanted and unwarranted thoughts and emotions on a regular basis. These are part of what it means to be human; it is the way we were created. I like to think that these moments of distraction are a constant reminder from the Creator that we are not as strong and in control as we like to think. In fact, we are quite fragile and dependent, especially in ways we might not imagine or easily accept.

That said, there is an essential difference between the non-scrupulous person and the scrupulous person in regard to these unwanted thoughts and emotions: the difference lies in how the individual interprets such experiences. The non-scrupulous person interprets such thoughts and emotions as distractions, momentary disruptions in life, and seldom gives such distractions another thought or care. On the other hand, the scrupulous person routinely interprets the same experiences as indicative of his or her personal choices and actions and assumes full responsibility for each disturbance. In addition, the scrupulous person embraces the presumed consequences of that responsibility as a serious matter, something potentially sinful and harmful to his or her relationship with God.

PART 2: CRITICAL BELIEFS

Because scrupulosity is also an anxiety disorder, unwanted thoughts and emotions trigger anxiety for the scrupulous. It is the anxious response—more than the thought, word, or action that triggered the anxiety—that the scrupulous person dreads most and wants, above all else, to avoid, subdue, or get rid of. That anxiety is the root manifestation of scrupulosity, and it is not a sin or a result of a bad decision.

Somewhat contrary to logic, the anxiety experienced by the scrupulous person is assurance that he or she did not freely generate or accept the unwanted thought or emotion. In short, when unwanted thoughts or emotions are accompanied by anxiety and consequently trigger the OCD ritual, no sin is possible from a moral standpoint, because the person's freedom is substantially diminished. The presence of anxiety is what differentiates someone with scrupulosity from someone without the affliction. For people without scrupulosity, distractions, no matter how powerful or vivid, carry no additional anxiety or distress. They are understood as normal human reactions with no assumed or imagined responsibility. Your experience of OCD and scrupulosity stands in stark contrast to this experience.

Another way to put this insight into context is to think about why someone would freely generate a thought, word, or action that produces a grievous emotion. People typically generate thoughts, words, or actions to produce pleasure, not to produce anxiety. There is a substantial difference between pleasure and anxiety, and it would be quite a stretch to proclaim that anxiety is pleasurable.

Some of you may respond to this by stating that your original intention of the thought, word, or action was for pleasure, but it quickly deteriorated into anxiety when you realized you were committing sin. This argument is indicative of the effects of scrupulosity and its ability to bend and shape an experience into something that fits neatly into the category of sin, even when it does not belong in that category.

As a scrupulous person, when you engage in this type of faulty reasoning, a good practice is to attempt to explain your train of thought—not as a result of sin, but as a result of your affliction—to someone without scrupulosity and see if he or she agrees with your interpretation. When the person disagrees with you, you may react by saying that he or she is not Catholic, is too liberal, completely misunderstands what you are saying, or something similar—this is an indication of your scrupulosity at work. The entire scenario demonstrates your diminished capacity due to scrupulosity; in no way are your unwanted thoughts or emotions sinful.

Two lessons can be learned from this reflection. First, all people, regardless of who they are, experience unwanted thoughts and emotions. It is part of the human condition and a sign of life, not a sign of sin. Second, when unwanted thoughts or emotions occur and produce anxiety, the anxiety itself is a sign that the person did not freely choose those thoughts or emotions. The anxiety is a very strong indication of the scrupulous affliction and a diminished capacity to choose freely. When there is diminished freedom, there is no sin. Although there may be strong anxiety, doubt, and many questions, there is no sin.

I have only one question, and when I get an answer, I will be just fine.

I have a very firm policy that I will not speak on the phone to anyone who calls me with a question about scrupulosity. Face-to-face interaction is a requirement when dealing with OCD. However, on one occasion, I broke my "ironclad policy" and agreed to talk on the phone with a caller who had scrupulosity. The caller worked very hard to connect with me, and she pleaded with me to answer "one simple question." Of course, I knew it was not going to be just one question, and despite my better judgment, I permitted her to ask it.

"I had a doubt, and I instinctively understood that the doubt was not clear and certain. Immediately after I experienced the doubt, I experienced a flood of doubts, and now I am all confused," she told me.

I told her that her instinct about the initial doubt was correct, and everything that occurred after that doubt was a manifestation of her OCD.

However, she insisted I didn't understand, so I explained again that she was engaging her OCD by the persistent questioning. She repeated that I didn't understand. Both of us became frustrated as the conversa-

PART 2: CRITICAL BELIEFS

tion repeated itself multiple times. After this unhelpful situation, I once again affirmed my decision to not engage in phone conversations about scrupulosity that are counterproductive and probably even harmful.

I have shared this anecdote with you in the hope that it might clarify why I and other priests might not accept calls from people who suffer with scrupulosity. It is not that we do not desire to help. On the contrary, such phone calls are counterproductive and do not help the scrupulous person. They only frustrate both parties and make it difficult to experience potential healing.

Healing can only happen when you refuse to act on the initial doubt. I know that sounds terrifying. I know it is a very big risk, and you often feel helpless and anxious. The only experience that is clear and certain in the entire OCD episodic manifestation is the first doubt that you instinctively understand as not being rooted in reality. Everything that takes place after that initial doubt is the fear, anxiety, and helplessness of OCD. To stop the OCD, you must trust your initial instinct and refuse to engage the doubt further.

God wants me to suffer with scrupulosity. It is the cross I am supposed to bear.

This is one of the mantras I occasionally hear from people with scrupulosity—one that I find puzzling and contradictory to my own understanding. This often-repeated perception suggests a deeply held belief that scrupulosity is something God intends to inflict on certain people as a test of their faith. As a result of this belief, some people feel they are required to undergo "patient suffering" and resist any remedy that might address their scrupulosity. This critical belief is reflective of an incorrect conclusion that to seek relief would be displeasing to God.

The Church does not teach that God inflicts suffering on his people. It is true that illness and suffering are consequences of the presence of sin in the world, but they are not wielded by God to punish the sinner. God does not single out men and women, randomly assigning them the pain and suffering of scrupulosity (or any other disease, for that matter).

It's more helpful to understand the Church's teaching that "illness and suffering have always been among the gravest problems confronted in human life," and that suffering provides humanity with an experience of "powerlessness, limitations, and finitude" (*CCC* 1500). While acknowledging the presence of suffering in the world, the Church also reminds people of faith that in the compassionate Christ we encounter in the gospels, we experience a resplendent sign: "God has visited his people" (Luke 7:16). Jesus "took away our infirmities and bore our diseases" (Matthew 8:17). Jesus is firmly on the side of the person who suffers; he is not the person who inflicted the suffering. (See *CCC* 1505.) Attempting to embrace this idea is well worth the effort. This new way of thinking removes some of the notion of victimization and offers a realistic hope that healing is possible.

In the Gospel of John, Chapter 5, the reader is invited to reflect on an encounter between Jesus and an ill man who reclines on a mat by the pool of Bethesda. The gospel story tells us that this man had been in the same place by the pool for many years. We are invited to imagine what might have motivated the man to endure his suffering and hope for relief. If we think about the story within the context of this reflection, we share a question that seems appropriate: Would this man continue to struggle day after day, despite the overwhelming odds against him to reach the pool and thereby be in a position to receive the healing power of Jesus' love, if he understood himself to be a victim? No. Without the man's struggle and desire to be healed, Jesus would have passed him by. If the man thought of himself as a victim, he would have remained in the shadows, feeling sorry for himself, and would never have experienced the healing he both required and desired.

Assuming the stance of "victim" is not patient suffering. Resisting any effort to seek help and not considering the possibility of relief are not virtuous. There is a tendency to become weary and give up hope after suffering for a prolonged period. There is also fear and anxiety associated with the risk of hoping. It is difficult to continue hoping for something in the face of overwhelming odds against you. Yet, if you don't take the risk, then healing will be impossible. Taking a leap of faith is a non-negotiable part of healing.

When scrupulous people fully engage in the process of healing, when they are willing to take responsibility for working with professionals who have the skills to help them, and when they experience suffering as part of the healing process, it is at that moment when pa-

PART 2: CRITICAL BELIEFS

tient suffering becomes a virtue. Exhibiting patience is an acknowledgement of the process and a realization that not all good things happen instantaneously. Often, the healing process is slow and deliberate, with progress marked in very small steps.

Thankfully, the Church invites people who are healing from illness to the sacrament of the anointing of the sick. It is appropriate for those who are suffering with scrupulosity and are truly "patiently suffering." As a healing sacrament, and as one of the sacraments of reconciliation, it can be a significant experience of God's grace. I often encourage people with scrupulosity to celebrate this sacrament whenever it is communally celebrated within their parish so that they can experience the grace of the sacrament. Many people have told me that this sacrament has become significant in their healing journey.

If you believe God is inflicting scrupulosity upon you, there is an appropriate and positive spiritual practice for you. It can be helpful to reorient your individual perception and understanding of your affliction. Ask God for the grace to actively participate in your personal journey of healing from scrupulosity. If you are burdened with an obstacle to your healing, such as believing that scrupulosity is God's will for you, ask to be freed from this incorrect belief.

Next, seek out the grace of the sacrament of the anointing of the sick as a dynamic expression of your personal belief in the healing power of the Lord. When you actively commit your energy and desire to the process of healing, the power of grace flows, and what you hope for often becomes a reality.

PART 2: CRITICAL BELIEFS

I have sinned so much in life that there is nothing and no one who can make me whole again.

The Apostle Paul, in his expansive and stirring letter to the Christian community in Rome, exclaims in a familiar passage, "For I am convinced that neither death, nor life, nor angels, nor principalities, nor present things, nor future things, nor powers, nor height, nor depth, nor any other creature will be able to separate us from the love of God in Christ Jesus our Lord" (Romans 8:38–39).

This proclamation is the summation of the Christian foundation of faith, captured also in the Gospel of John: "For God so loved the world that he gave his only Son" (John 3:16). The *Catechism* also states, "The Word became flesh so that thus we might know God's love" (*CCC* 458).

Because we are loved by God, and because God's love for us is eternal, we should reflect often on these hopeful words of Paul, especially during those moments when we feel alone and alienated. It is particularly reassuring to know and understand that God loves us at this moment, at this time, exactly as we are, and not as we one day might be.

A Guide for the Scrupulous

If, rather, we suffer from the illusion of separation from God, we will be deprived of this essential experience of God's love—not because God has somehow stopped loving us but because of our own perception, our own lives tainted by scrupulosity. We need to understand that this deprivation is not real; it is an illusion rooted in our experiences of fear, guilt, and anxiety, emotions that rob and deprive us of the truth of God's love for us.

Such emotions construct a parallel reality that keeps us unsettled and makes life difficult. This parallel reality tells us there is something that can separate us from the love of Christ, which is contrary to the teaching of Paul. This parallel reality is also particularly devastating because it robs the sufferer from any real possibility of Christ's peace. The pain and suffering that results are associated with scrupulosity.

Unfortunately, if you suffer from this illusion, there is no simple way to release yourself from the illusion and get on the path to knowing you are loved. The recommendations from your confessor, counselor, or others who offer you support are helpful, but they do not offer a final, satisfactory result. You require something more.

One potential solution comes from using your imag-

PART 2: CRITICAL BELIEFS

ination to dwell on positive possibilities and taking small steps toward achieving those outcomes. When you employ the gift of imagination God has given all of us, you can improve your response to life by imagining yourself as "more"—more trustworthy, more fit and trim, more relaxed. When these positive outcomes are the intended result of your imagination, and you put into action a plan that enables slow and patient movement toward what you have imagined, more often than not, you will experience real growth. If, on the other hand, you are unable to imagine what you hope for, then you will become discouraged from even attempting an effort.

Over the years, I have been involved in vocational discernment with men and women who believe they have a vocation to the priesthood or religious life. I have learned to value and appreciate the necessity of the role of imagination in the discernment process. If a person is unable to imagine serving and living as a priest, sister, or brother, this usually ends the discussion. This is not much different from the process a person uses for other vocational discernments, such as becoming a lawyer or a doctor. The imagination fuels the possibility of the dream becoming a reality.

For you, a scrupulous person, it is important to imagine what life might feel like if you are convinced that you cannot be separated from the love of God. After all, scrupulous people spend countless hours imagining what it is like to be separated from God and dwelling on the dire consequences of this reality. Why not reverse the process and imagine the best possible situation? How energizing and freeing it might be to see yourself confident about the power of your relationship with God and secure in God's love for you every day. That reality can put a bounce in your step and make difficult challenges easier to carry.

Return to the words of Paul and read them daily. Reread this reflection frequently. How wonderful it would be to anchor your day in the revelation that there is nothing that can separate you from the love of Christ.

PART 3

HELPFUL PRAYERS

Note: I hope this section that suggests helpful prayers will be useful to our readers, but I would be remiss in my instructions if I did not emphasize the most important part of prayer: engaging the relationship or, perhaps better yet, showing up. Choosing to be present at prayer rather than engaging in some other activity is in itself a grace, a gift from God that is not to be ignored or underestimated. It is your response to the gift of the Holy Spirit, who has called you to prayer. What happens in prayer—or, for that matter, what does not happen—is secondary to showing up.

It does not matter what form your prayer takes. It can be contemplative; it can be liturgical; it can be intercessory; it can take many different forms, each dependent on the first and most important step: **showing up.** Forming the habit and maintaining the discipline of showing up for prayer is essential. Count it as grace. Accept it as a gift. Refrain from judging it in any shape or form. Just be grateful that you said "yes" to the call.

Meditations on the Eucharist by Saint Alphonsus Liguori

What is true love? Is true love something that permeates all, commands all attention, influences every decision, and colors every thought? Can an experience of true love be found, or is it the stuff of fantasy and fairy tales, something we read about but is not actually possible? Is true love something we should hope for, only to become frustrated and disappointed in the pursuit?

When you read the meditations, prayers, and affections gathered here, you will know that true love is possible. You will read about a love for Jesus present in the most holy Communion. You will recognize a love and devotion that is all consuming, that is never doubted, and that explodes in every thought, affection, and prayer. Saint Alphonsus is possessed by the true love of Jesus in the Eucharist!

True love such as this is contagious. It would have been enjoyable to witness St. Alphonsus praying before the tabernacle and meditating on the truths of his relationship with God. The experience would have inspired greater prayer and devotion in us. We experience something similar when in the presence of two people in love, whether newlyweds or those weathered by years of practice, because we sense their love and can become inspired to love more deeply those around us.

If we could have been with St. Alphonsus as he prayed, we would have sensed something during the experience and come out the better for it. Unfortunately, we cannot pray with St. Alphonsus in the presence of the Eucharist today. We can, however, catch something of his spirit in the meditations and affections presented here. In this small way, we might possibly experience something of the all-consuming love and devotion he felt for the Eucharist. From this, we can begin to form an answer to the question, "What is true love?"

First Meditation:
The Love of Jesus in the Most Holy Sacrament

Our loving Redeemer, knowing that he must leave this earth and return to his Father as soon as he had accomplished the work of our redemption by his death, and seeing that the hour of his death had come—"Jesus knew that his hour had come to pass from this world to the Father" (John 13:1)—would not leave us alone in this valley of tears. What did he do? He instituted the most holy sacrament of the Eucharist, in which he left us his whole self. "No tongue," said St. Peter of Alcantara, "is able to declare the greatness of the love that Jesus bears for every soul." Therefore, this Spouse, as he left this earth, in order that his absence might not cause us to forget him, gave us as a memorial: this Blessed Sacrament, in which he himself remained. He would not have any other pledge than himself to keep alive our remembrance of him.

Jesus would not be separated from us by his death; he instituted this sacrament of love in order to be with us to the end of the world: "I am with you always, until the end of the age" (Matthew 28:20). Behold him, as faith teaches us, on so many altars as in so many prisons of love. Behold him, in order that he may be found by everyone who seeks him. "But, O Lord," says St. Bernard, "this does not demonstrate your majesty." Jesus Christ answers, "It is enough that it demonstrates my love."

People feel great tenderness and devotion when they go to Jerusalem and visit the cave where the Incarnate Word was born, the hall where he was scourged, the hill of Calvary on which he died, and the tomb where he was buried. How much greater should our tenderness be when we visit an altar on which Jesus remains in the most holy sacrament! The Venerable Fr. John Ávila used to say that of all sanctuaries, there is not one to be found more excellent and devout than a church where Jesus is sacramentally present.

Affections and Prayers

O my beloved Jesus, O God, who has loved me with love exceeding! What more can you do to make yourself loved by ungrateful people? If we loved you, all the churches would be continually filled with people prostrate on the ground, adoring and thanking you, burning with love for you and seeing you with the eyes of faith, hidden in a tabernacle. But no, we are forgetful of you and your love. We are ready enough to try to win the favor of a person from whom we hope for some miserable advantage, while we leave you, Lord, abandoned and alone. If only by my devotion I could make reparation for such ingratitude! I am sorry that I have also been careless and ungrateful. In the future, I will change my ways; I will devote myself to your service as much as possible. Inflame me with your holy love so that from this day forward I may live only to love and to please you. You deserve the love of all hearts. If at one time I have despised you, I now desire nothing but to love you. O my Jesus, you are my love and my only good, "My God and my all."

Most holy Virgin Mary, obtain for me, I pray, a great love for the most holy sacrament.

Second Meditation:
Jesus Remains on the Altar So That All May Find Him

Saint Teresa of Ávila said that in this world, it is impossible for all subjects to speak to their king. For the poor, the most they can hope for is to speak to him with the help of a third party. But to speak to you, O King of heaven, there is no need of a third person. Everyone who wishes can find you in the most holy sacrament and can speak to you at their convenience and without conditions. For this reason, the same saint states that Jesus Christ has concealed his majesty in the sacrament, under the appearance of bread, to give us more confidence and to take away our fear of approaching him.

Jesus seems continually to exclaim from the altar, "Come to me, all you who labor and are burdened, and I will give you rest" (Matthew 11:28). "Come," he says, "come you who are poor; come, you who are infirm;

PART 3: HELPFUL PRAYERS

come, you who are afflicted; come, you who are just and you who are sinners; and you shall find in me a remedy for all your losses and afflictions." This is the desire of Jesus Christ: to console every person who calls upon him.

Jesus remains day and night on our altars so that he may be found by all and so that he may grant favors to all. The saints experienced in this world such pleasure in remaining in the presence of Jesus in the Blessed Sacrament that days and nights appeared to them as moments. The Countess of Feria, having become a nun of the Order of St. Clare, never tired of remaining in the chapel in sight of the tabernacle. One day, she was asked what she was doing for so long before the most holy sacrament. She answered with surprise, "What do I do before the Blessed Sacrament? What do I do? I return thanks, I love, and I pray!" Saint Philip Neri, while in the presence of the Eucharist, exclaimed, "Behold my love, behold all of my love." If Jesus meant to us what he meant to the saints, then days and nights in his presence would appear to us as moments.

Affections and Prayers

O my Jesus, from this day forward, I also hope to say

always to you, when I come to visit you on your altar, "Behold my love, behold all of my love!" Yes, my beloved Redeemer, I will love only you and I desire that you should be the only love of my soul. I seem to die of sorrow when I think that until this moment, I have loved creatures and my own pleasures more than you. I have turned my back on you, the ultimate good. But you would not permit me to be lost, and therefore you have been patient with me. Instead of chastising me, you have pierced my heart with darts of love so that I could no longer resist your kindness. But now that I have freely given myself to you, I see that you desire me to be entirely yours. For this desire to be fulfilled, you must make it possible. You must detach my heart from all earthly affections and from myself. You must enable me to seek no other but you, that I may think only of you, and that I may only desire to burn with love for you and to live and die for you alone. O love of my Jesus, come and occupy my whole heart and expel from it all other love but that of God! I love you, Jesus in the sacrament; I love you, my treasure, my love, my all.

O Mary, my hope. Pray for me and make me belong entirely to Jesus.

PART 3: HELPFUL PRAYERS

Third Meditation:
The Great Gift Jesus Has Given to Us Through His Presence in the Blessed Sacrament

The love of Jesus Christ was not satisfied with sacrificing his divine life for us. He sacrificed himself in the midst of a sea of humiliations and torments. He sacrificed himself to prove to us his affection. He sacrificed himself to oblige us to love him even more. He sacrificed himself so that on the night before his death, he left us his whole self as our food in the holy Eucharist. God is omnipotent, but after he has given himself to a soul in this sacrament of love, he has nothing more to give. The Council of Trent teaches that Jesus, in giving himself to us in holy Communion, pours forth all the riches of his infinite love in this gift: "He has, as it were, poured forth the treasures of his love toward us."

How would the servant react, writes St. Francis de Sales, if his master, while he was eating, would send him a portion from his own plate? Would he not consider himself blessed and esteemed? Jesus, in this holy

Communion, gives us for our food not only a portion of his own meal, but all his body: "Take and eat; this is my body" (Matthew 26:26). And together with his body, he gives us also his soul and divinity. Saint John Chrysostom says that our Lord, in giving himself to us in the Blessed Sacrament, gives us all that he has and nothing more remains: "He gave all to you, and left nothing for himself." O wonderful prodigy of divine love, that God, who is Lord of all, makes himself entirely ours!

Affections and Prayers

O my dear Jesus, what can you do to make me love you? Make me understand what an excess of love you have shown me by reducing yourself to food in order to unite yourself to poor sinners! You, my dear Redeemer, have so much affection for me that you have not refused to give yourself again and again entirely to me in holy Communion. And yet I have had the courage to drive you away from my soul on so many occasions! You do not despise a humble and contrite heart. You became human for my sake. You died for me. You even went so far as to become my food. What more can there remain for you to do to gain my love? Oh, that I could die with grief every time that I remember that I have despised your grace. I repent, O my love, with my whole heart for having offended you. I love you, O Infinite Goodness! I love you, O Infinite Love! I desire nothing but to love you, and I fear nothing but to live without your love. My beloved Jesus, do not refuse to come to me. Come, because I would rather die a thousand times than drive you away again. I will do all that I can to please you. Come and inflame my whole soul with your love. Grant that I may forget everything, to think only of you, and to desire you alone, my Sovereign and my only good.

O Mary, my Mother, pray for me, and by your prayers make me grateful for all the love that Jesus has for me.

Fourth Meditation:
The Great Love Jesus Has Shown Us in the Blessed Sacrament

"Jesus knew that his hour had come to pass from this world to the Father. He loved his own in the world and he loved them to the end" (John 13:1). Jesus, knowing that his hour had come, desired to leave us, before he died, the greatest pledge of his affection that he could give us—the gift of the most holy sacrament. St. John Chrysostom explains "He loved them to the end," as "He loved them with extreme love." Jesus loved us with the greatest love with which he could love us by giving us his entire self.

When did Jesus institute this great sacrament, the sacrament in which he has left us himself? On the night before he died! "The Lord Jesus, on the night he was handed over, took bread, and, after he had given thanks, broke it and said, 'This is my body that is for you. Do this in remembrance of me'" (1 Corinthians 11:23–24). At the precise moment that his enemies were plotting to put him to death, he gave us this last proof of his love.

The words of affection that we receive from our friends at the time of their death remain deeply impressed on our hearts. For this reason, Jesus gave us this gift of the Blessed Sacrament just before his death. With reason did St. Thomas call this gift "a sacrament and pledge of love." Saint Bernard describes it as "the love of loves." Saint Mary Magdalene de'Pazzi called the day on which Jesus instituted this sacrament "the day of love." In this sacrament, Jesus united and accomplished all the other acts of love that he had shown us.

PART 3: HELPFUL PRAYERS

Affections and Prayers

O infinite love of Jesus, worthy of being loved with infinite love. My Lord, you love me so much; how is it that I can love you so little in return? O my Jesus, you are so amiable and so loving. Make yourself known; make yourself loved. When shall I love you as you have loved me? Help me to discover more and more the greatness of your mercy, in order that I may burn more and more with your love and always seek to please you. Beloved of my soul, I wish that I had always loved you. Regretfully, there was a time when I not only did not love you, but when I also despised your grace and your love! I am consoled by the sorrow that I now feel, and I hope to be reconciled because of your promise to forgive those who repent of their sins. To you, my Savior, do I give all my affections. Help me, through the merits of your passion, to love you with my whole strength. If only I could die for you, as you died for me!

O Mary, my mother, obtain for me the grace to love God alone.

Fifth Meditation:
The Soul United With Jesus in Holy Communion

Saint Dionysius the Areopagite teaches that the principal effect of love is the union of those who are in love. For this purpose, Jesus instituted holy Communion, so that he might unite himself entirely to our souls. He had given himself to us as our teacher, our example, and our victim. All that remained was for him to give himself to us as our food, that he might become one with us, as food becomes one with the person who eats it. Jesus did this by instituting this sacrament of love. Saint Bernardine of Siena says, "The last degree of love is when Jesus gave himself to us to be our food, uniting with us in every way."

Jesus was not satisfied with this unity with our human nature, but he would, by this sacrament, find a way to unite himself to each one of us. In this way, Jesus makes himself one with the person who receives him in the sacrament. Saint Francis de Sales writes, "In no other action can our Savior be considered more tender or more loving than in this, in which he, as it were, annihilates himself and reduces himself to food, that he may penetrate our souls and unite himself to the hearts of the faithful."

PART 3: HELPFUL PRAYERS

Because Jesus loves us so much, he desires to unite himself to us in the holy Eucharist, we might become the same thing with him. Saint John Chrysostom writes, "He mingled himself with us, that we might be one, for this belongs to those who love greatly." Jesus wills, in short, that our hearts and his heart should form one heart. "He wills that we should have one heart with him," prays St. Lawrence Justinian.

Our Savior himself said this: "The one who feeds on me will have life because of me" (John 6:57). Whoever receives holy Communion has life from Jesus, and Jesus lives in them. This union is not mere affection but is a true and real union. "As two candles, when melted," says St. Cyril of Alexandria, "unite themselves into one, so the person that communicates becomes one with Jesus Christ." Let us therefore imagine, when we receive holy Communion, that Jesus says to us that which he said one day to his beloved servant, Margaret of Ypres: "Behold, my daughter, the beautiful union between me and you. Come, then, love me, and let us remain constantly united in love, never more to be separated."

Affections and Prayers

O my Jesus, this is what I seek of you and what I will always seek for you in holy Communion: "Let us be always united, and never more to be separate." I know that you will not separate yourself from me if I do not first separate myself from you. But this is my fear, that I should in the future separate myself from you by sin, as I have done in the past. O my most blessed Redeemer, do not permit it. Let me never be separated from you. As long as I am alive, I am in danger of this. Through the merits of your death, I beg you to let me die rather than be separated from you again.

O God of my soul, I love you, I love you. I will always love you and you alone. I swear before heaven and earth that I desire you alone and nothing but you. O my Jesus, hear me. I desire you alone and nothing but you.

O Mary, Mother of mercy, pray for me now and obtain for me the grace never more to separate myself from Jesus, and to love only Jesus.

Sixth Meditation:
The Desire That Jesus Has to Unite Himself to Us in Holy Communion

"Jesus knew that his hour had come" (John 13:1). This hour, which Jesus called "his hour," was the hour of the night in which his passion was to begin. Why did he call so sad an hour "his hour"? Because this was the hour he had prepared for his whole life. It was in this hour that he determined to leave us the sacrament of the holy Eucharist. It was in this hour and in this sacrament that he desired to unite himself entirely to the souls whom he loved and for whom he was soon to give his blood and his life.

Recall how he spoke on that night to his disciples: "I have eagerly desired to eat this Passover with you" (Luke 22:15). With these words, he expresses his desire and anxiousness to unite himself to us in this sacrament of love. Saint Lawrence Justinian states that these words were words that came from the heart of Jesus. His heart burned with infinite love: "This is the voice of passionate love."

The same flame that burned in the heart of Jesus on that blessed night burns in his heart today. Jesus gives the same invitation to receive him to all of us today as he gave to his apostles on that night: "Take and eat; this is my body" (Matthew 26:26). To entice us to receive him with affection, he promises paradise: "Whoever eats my flesh and drinks my blood remains in me and I in him" (John 6:56). If we refuse to receive him, he threatens us with death: "Unless you eat the flesh of the Son of Man and drink his blood, you do not have life within you" (John 6:53).

These invitations, promises, and threats all find their source in the desire of Jesus Christ to unite himself to us in holy Communion through the love he has for us. "There is not a bee," said our Lord to St. Mechtilde, "which seeks the honey out of the flowers with such eagerness of delight, as I have to enter into the souls that desire me." Jesus, because he loves us, desires to be loved by us. Because he desires us, he wishes that we desire him in return. "God thirsts to be thirsted after," writes St. Gregory. Blessed is that soul that approaches holy Communion with a great desire to be united to Jesus Christ.

Affections and Prayers

My adorable Jesus, you cannot give me greater proof of your love to show me how much you love me. You have given your life for me. You have willed yourself to me in the holy sacrament, in order that I may come and nourish myself with your Body and Blood. You are anxious that I will receive you. How, then, can I become aware of all these proofs of your love and not burn with love for you? All earthly affections, leave my heart, you hinder me from burning with love for Jesus as he burns with love for me. What other pledges of love can I expect, my beloved Redeemer, than those which you have already given me? You have sacrificed your whole life for my love. You have embraced for my sake a bitter and infamous death. You have reduced yourself almost to annihilation by becoming food in the holy Eucharist to give yourself entirely to us. O Lord, let me no longer live ungrateful for such great goodness.

I thank you for having given me time to repent of the offenses I have committed against you and to love you during these days that remain to me in this life. I repent for having despised your love. I love you, O Infinite Goodness! I love you, O Infinite Treasure! I love you, O Infinite Love who are worthy of infinite love! O, help me, my Jesus, to discard from my heart all affections that are not directed to you so that from this day forward I may not desire, nor seek, nor love any other but you.

My beloved Lord, grant that I may always find you and grant that I may always love you. Take possession of my whole will, in order that I may never desire anything except that which is pleasing to you. My God, my God, whom shall I love, if I do not love you, who are the Supreme Good? I do indeed desire you, and nothing more.

O Mary, my Mother, take my heart into your keeping and fill it with pure love for Jesus Christ.

Seventh Meditation:
Holy Communion Obtains for Us Perseverance in Divine Grace

When Jesus comes to the soul in holy Communion, he brings to the soul every grace, and specifically the grace of holy perseverance. This is the principal effect of the most holy sacrament of the altar: to nourish the soul that receives it with this food of life and to give it great strength to advance in perfection and resist those enemies who desire our death. For this reason, Jesus identifies himself in this sacrament: "I am the living bread that came down from heaven; whoever eats this bread will live forever" (John 6:51). Even as earthly bread sustains the life of the body, so too this heavenly bread sustains the life of the soul by making it persevere in the grace of God.

The Council of Trent teaches that holy Communion is the remedy that delivers us from daily faults and preserves us from mortal sins. Pope Innocent III writes that Jesus Christ, through his passion, delivers us from sins committed, and by the holy Eucharist, from sins that we might commit. Saint Bonaventure says that sinners must not keep away from Communion because they have been sinners; on the contrary, for this very reason they should receive Communion more frequently: "The more infirm a person feels, the more that person is in need of a doctor."

Affections and Prayers

Miserable sinner that I am, O Lord, how do I lament my weakness when I consider my many falls from grace? How was it possible for me to resist the assaults of the devil while I stayed away from you, who are my strength? If I had more often approached you in holy Communion, I would not have been overcome by my enemies. In the future, I will not repeat this mistake. "In you, LORD, I take refuge; let me never be put to shame" (Psalm 31:2). I will no longer rely on my own strength. You alone are my hope, O my Jesus. You will give me strength so that I will no longer fall into sin. I am weak, but through holy Communion, you will make me strong against every temptation: "I have the strength for everything through him who empowers me" (Philippians 4:13).

Forgive me, Jesus, of all the offenses that I have committed against you and from which I repent with my whole heart. I resolve never to offend you again. I trust in your passion, that you will give me your help to perse-

vere in your grace to the end of my life. "My God, in you I trust; do not let me be disgraced" (Psalm 25:2).

With St. Bonaventure, I will say the same to you, O Mary, my Mother: "In you, O Lady, I trust; I shall not be disgraced."

Eighth Meditation:
Preparation for Communion and Thanksgiving After Communion

Cardinal Bona asks, "Why is it that so many souls, after so many Communions, make so little progress in the way of God?" He answers his question by stating that "the fault is not in the food, but rather in the disposition of the person who receives it." In other words, there is not sufficient preparation on the part of the communicant. Fire quickly burns dry wood but not wood that is green, because the green wood is not fit to burn. The saints derived great profit from their Communions because they were very careful in their preparation for the reception of the sacrament.

There are two principal things that we should endeavor to obtain to prepare ourselves for holy Communion and to gain the greatest fruit.

The first is detachment from creatures, driving from our heart everything that is not of God and for God. Although the soul may be in a state of grace, if the heart is occupied by other things, then the more there is of the earth in the soul, and thus less room will there be for the fire of divine love. Saint Gertrude once asked our Lord what preparation he required of her for holy Communion. Jesus answered, "I require nothing more from you except that you come to receive me not full of yourself."

The second thing that is necessary to harvest the greatest fruit from Communion is the desire to receive Jesus Christ with the intention of loving him more. Gerson says that at the Eucharistic banquet, no one is filled except those who feel great hunger. Saint Francis de Sales writes that the principal intention of a soul receiving Communion should be to grow in the love of God: "He should be received for love because it is out of pure love that he gives himself to us." Saint Mechtilde writes that our Lord told her, "When you are going to communicate, desire all the love that any soul ever had for me, and I will receive it according to the desire, as if it were your own."

It is also highly recommended to make a thanksgiving after Communion. There is no prayer dearer to God than the prayer made after Communion. We must occupy this time in acts of love and prayers. The devout acts of love that we make at this time have greater merit in the sight of God. Our acts at this time are animated by the presence of Jesus Christ, who is united to our souls. Saint Teresa says that Jesus, after Communion, remains in the soul as on a throne of grace and says to the soul, "What is it that you hope that I do for you?" The Lord invites us to ask for as much as we need and to be assured that we will be heard. What treasures of grace do people lose who pray a short time to God after holy Communion!

Affections and Prayers

O God of love, you desire to grant favors to me, and yet I seem to be uninterested in receiving them. What sorrow will I feel at the hour of my death, when I think of this negligence, so pernicious to my soul! O my Lord, forget, I implore you, all that is in my past. In the future, with your help, I will better prepare myself. I will try to detach my affections from everything that prevents me from receiving all those graces that you desire to give to me. After Communion, I will lift up my heart to you as much as I can, in order to obtain your help so that I may grow in love for you. Grant me the grace to accomplish this!

O my Jesus, how negligent have I been in loving you. The time that you, in your mercy, give to me in this life is the time to prepare myself for death and to make amends for the offenses I have committed against you. I will spend my time on earth lamenting my sins and loving you. I love you, Jesus my love; I love you, my only good; have pity on me and do not forsake me.

Mary, my hope, do not cease to help me by your holy intercession!

PART 3: HELPFUL PRAYERS

Helpful Prayers from Various Religious Traditions

For some readers, including prayers from other spiritual traditions may seem unwise and unhelpful. Their inclusion here is not intended for any other reason than to provide comforting words that may help a person grow in his or her relationship with God. The Christian tradition, specifically the Roman Catholic spiritual tradition, is always open to the heartfelt expressions of belief by men and women of many faith traditions. Their words may be unfamiliar, but they express an experience of God familiar to all people of faith, regardless of religious tradition.

A Guide for the Scrupulous

I asked God for strength, that I might achieve.
I was made weak, that I might learn humbly to obey.

I asked for health, that I might do great things,
I was given infirmity, that I might do better things.

I asked for riches, that I might be happy.
I was given poverty, that I might be wise.

I asked for power, that I might have the praise of men.
I was given weakness, that I might feel the need for God.

I asked for all things, that I might enjoy life,
I was given life, that I might enjoy all things.

I got nothing that I asked for,
    but everything that I hoped for.
Almost despite myself, my unspoken prayers
    were answered.

I am, among all men, richly blessed.

Prayer by Henry Viscardi, Jr. (1912–2004)
Disability Rights Advocate

PART 3: HELPFUL PRAYERS

Father, I abandon myself into your hands;
> do with me what you will.

Whatever you may do, I thank you:
> I am ready for all, I accept all.

Let only your will be done in me and in all your creatures.

I wish no more than this, Lord.

Into your hands I commend my soul:

I offer it all to you with all the love of my heart,

For I love you, Lord, and so need to give myself,

To surrender myself into your hands without reserve,

And with boundless confidence, for you are my Father.

> Prayer of Abandonment by St. Charles de Foucauld
> (1858–1916) Trappist Monk

A Guide for the Scrupulous

Lord, my God, teach my heart where and how to seek
you, and where and how to find you.

O Lord, you are my God and my Lord,
and I have never seen you.

You have made me and remade me, and you have
bestowed on me all the good things I possess,

And still I do not know you!

I have not yet done that for which I was made.

Teach me to seek you, for I cannot seek you
unless you show yourself to me.

Let me seek you in my desire,
let me desire you in my seeking.

Let me find you by loving you,
let me love you when I find you.

> Prayer by St. Anselm of Canterbury (1033–1109)
> Doctor of the Church

PART 3: HELPFUL PRAYERS

Lord, catch me off guard today.

Surprise me with some moment of beauty or pain,

So that at least for the moment,

I may be startled into seeing that you are here
in all your splendor,

Always and everywhere,

Barely hidden,

Beneath,

Beyond,

Within this life I breathe.

Prayer by Frederick Buechner (1926–2022)
Presbyterian Minister and Theologian

Late have I loved you, O Beauty, ever ancient, ever new.

Late have I loved you.

For behold you were within me, and I outside.

And I sought you outside,

And in my unloveliness fell upon those lovely things that you had made.

You were with me, and I was not with you.

I was kept from you by those,

Yet had they not been in you,

They would not have been at all.

You did call and cry to me to break open my deafness,

And you did send forth your beams to shine upon me,

And chase away my blindness.

You breathed fragrance upon me,

And I drew my breath and do now pant for you.

I tasted you and now hunger and thirst for you.

You touched me, and I burn for you.

Prayer by St. Augustine (354–430)
Doctor of the Church

PART 3: HELPFUL PRAYERS

O you who dwell in the house made of the dawn,
In the house made of the evening twilight…
Where the dark mist curtains the doorway,
The path to which is on the rainbow…
I have made your sacrifice.
I have prepared a smoke for you.

My feet restore for me.
My limbs restore for me.
My body restore for me.
My mind restore for me.
My voice restore for me.

Today, take away your spell from me.
Away from me you have taken it.
Far off from me you have taken it.

Happily I recover.
Happily my interior becomes cool.
Happily my eyes regain their power.
Happily my head becomes cool.

Happily my limbs regain their power.

Happily I hear again.

Happily for me the spell is taken off.

Happily I walk.

Impervious to pain, I walk.

Feeling light within, I walk…

In beauty I walk.

With beauty before me, I walk.

With beauty behind me, I walk.

With beauty below me, I walk.

With beauty all around me, I walk.

It is finished in beauty.

It is finished in beauty.

It is finished in beauty.

From Night Chant, a Navajo Indian Prayer

PART 3: HELPFUL PRAYERS

Allah, there is no God but he, the Living, the Eternal.

Neither slumber nor sleep seizes him.

To him belongs what is in the heavens
    and in the earth.

Who can intercede with him, except by his permission?

He knows what lies before them and after them,

And they know nothing of his knowledge,
    save such as he wills.

His throne encompasses the heavens and the earth,

And he never wearies of preserving them.

He is Sublime, the Exalted.

> Holy Qur'an, Surat al-Baqarah, Ayat al Kursi
> (Verse of the Throne)

A Guide for the Scrupulous

May the kingdom of justice prevail!

May the believers be united in love!

May the hearts of the believers be humble,
 high their wisdom,

And may they be guided in their wisdom by the Lord.

Glory be to God!

Entrust unto the Lord what thou wishest
 to be accomplished.

The Lord will bring all matters to fulfillment.

Know this as truth evidenced by himself.

SIKH PRAYER FOR ABUNDANCE

All that is in the heavens and the earth glorify God;

And he is the Mighty, the wise.

He is the Sovereignty of the heavens and the earth;

He is able to do all things.

He is the First and the Last,

And the Outward and the Inward;

He is the knower of all things.

HOLY QUR'AN, AL-HADID, VERSES 1–3

PART 3: HELPFUL PRAYERS

O gracious and holy Father,

Give us wisdom to perceive you,

Intelligence to understand you,

Diligence to seek you,

Patience to wait for you,

Eyes to see you,

A heart to meditate on you,

And a life to proclaim you,

Through the power of the spirit
   of Jesus Christ our Lord.

> Prayer by St. Benedict (480–547)
> Founder of Modern Monasticism

A Guide for the Scrupulous

Those who know do not speak;

Those who speak do not know.

Stop up the openings,

Close down the doors,

Rub off the sharp edges.

Unravel all confusion.

Harmonize the light,

Give up the contention:

This is called finding the unity of life.

When love and hatred cannot affect you,

Profit and loss cannot touch you,

Praise and blame cannot ruffle you,

You are honored by all the world.

MEDITATION BY LAO TZU
(CA. 6TH CENTURY BC–5TH CENTURY BC)
CHINESE PHILOSOPHER

PART 3: HELPFUL PRAYERS

God, I love your creativity,

The way you can fill an ordinary day
 with momentous experiences;

Your ability to turn a bad situation
 into an occasion for growth;

Your mercy, which transforms episodes of sin
 into encounters with salvation.

I love your affinity for beauty.

I love your sense of humor.

I love your steadfast presence.

I love your vulnerability.

I love your comfort.

I love your commitment to community.

I love your favor for underdogs.

I love your passion for ministry, for peace,
 and for revelation.

I love what you do and who you are.

I love you for being you, God!

> Prayer by Rev. Dr. C. Weldon Gaddy (1942–2023)
> Baptist Pastor

A Guide for the Scrupulous

Almighty Lord, if we offer you a devoted mind and heart, you will offer to us every blessing on earth and in heaven. You grant our deepest wishes. You give food to the body and peace to the soul. You look upon us with the love of a mother for her children.

You created this beautiful earth all around us. And in every plant and animal, every tree and bird, your spirit dwells. You have revealed yourself to me, infusing my soul with the knowledge that you are the source of all blessing. And so I sing your praises day and night. I who am feeble, glorify you who are powerful. I who am nothing, devote myself to you who are everything.

DIVINE BLESSING FROM THE *ATHARVA VEDA*

PART 3: HELPFUL PRAYERS

Supreme God, your light is brighter than the sun, your purity whiter than mountain snow, you are present wherever I go. All people of wisdom praise you. So, I too put faith in all your words, knowing that everything you teach is true. Neither the angels in heaven nor the demons in hell can know the perfection of your wisdom, for it is beyond all understanding. Only your Spirit knows you; only you can know your true self. You are the source of all being, the power of all power, the ruler of all creatures. So, you alone understand what you are. In your mercy reveal to me all that I need to know, in order to find peace and joy. Tell me the truths that are necessary for the world in which I live.

Show me how I can meditate upon you, learning from you the wisdom that I need. I am never tired of hearing you, because your words bring life.

From *Bhagavad Gita* ("The Song of God")

A Guide for the Scrupulous

The Holy Spirit: living and life-giving,
   the life that's all things moving,
   the root in all created being:
   of filth and muck it washes all things clean—
   out-scrubbing guilty staining,
   its balm our wounds constraining—
   and so its life with praise is shining,
   rousing and reviving all.

O Shepherd of souls
   and o first voice
   through whom all creation was summoned,
   now to you,
   to you may it give pleasure and dignity
   to liberate us
   from our miseries and languishing.
        Prayer by St. Hildegard of Bingen (1098–1179)

Beloved God,

Show me the truth about this.

I now surrender all fears, doubts, and judgments,

PART 3: HELPFUL PRAYERS

And invite the light of perfect consciousness
    to illuminate my path.
Pure love is present here and now,
    as God lives in every person I meet.
I send love and appreciation to all my associates,
Knowing with perfect confidence,
That he or she is guided by the same great Spirit
    that guides me.
I am not separate from my brothers and sisters
    but one with them.
I trust that my highest good is unfolding before me,
And I accept the very best that love and life have to offer.
I am worthy of living in the kingdom of heaven,
    even as I walk the earth.
I claim it now.
Thank you, God, for loving me infinitely,
And opening all doors for the highest good
    of all concerned.
I receive your love and magnify it.
And so it is.

Prayer by Alan Cohen (1950–)
Christian Author

A Practical Model for Entering Into Prayer

"Speak, for your servant is listening."

1 SAMUEL 3:10

1. Choose a specific and suitable place to pray, a place where you feel comfortable and will experience the fewest interruptions.

2. Take a moment to become relaxed. Become aware of the rhythm of your breathing and permit the rhythm to slowly calm you and free you from the anxiety and concerns of the day.

3. With each inhale, permit the Spirit of God to enter into you. With each exhale, let go of concerns, worry, and anxiety.

4. Recall the presence of God and let that presence be gently with you.

5. Permit your thoughts to simply flow past, not unlike a river that passes before you.

PART 3: HELPFUL PRAYERS

6. Enter into the silence and let it be present to you.

7. When you feel ready, slowly become aware of other sounds around you and gently permit the silence to recede, fully aware that you can return again in prayer.

8. Rest for a moment before you return to the thoughts and concerns of the day.

On those occasions when the silence may be difficult to experience or when you are in need of specific direction or inspiration, Step 6 can include the meditative reading of Scripture or the words of a spiritual mentor. Read only a small section, pausing and reflecting on a single word or thought that may capture your imagination. When you are ready, return to the silence for at least a moment before moving on to Step 7.

Favorite Scripture Passages for Prayer

Scripture passages often present us with an opportunity to pray with another, to join our thoughts with another's thoughts. Even though the feelings and hopes expressed are thousands of years old, they nevertheless succeed in adequately describing our special needs and desires today. Such prayers are also useful as a springboard for our own prayer.

Isaiah 43:1–7	*You are precious in my eyes.*
1 Samuel 3:1–18	*Speak, for your servant is listening.*
Psalm 40	*I delight to do your will, my God.*
Psalm 42	*My soul thirsts for God, the living God.*
Psalm 51	*Have mercy on me, God.*
Psalm 139	*You formed my inmost being.*
Wisdom 11:21–27	*For you love all things that are.*
Luke 1:46–55	*My soul proclaims the greatness of the Lord.*
Ephesians 2:11–18	*For through him we both have access in one Spirit to the Father.*
Romans 8:28–39	*We conquer overwhelmingly through him who loved us.*

PART 3: HELPFUL PRAYERS

Sometimes, when we come to prayer, we may experience a dominant thought or feeling that is immediately present to us. It is often useful to acknowledge such strong feelings or thoughts instead of ignoring them or pushing them aside. There is an operating assumption that the presence of a strong preference may well be the voice of God or the call of the Holy Spirit.

Trust
Luke 1:26–38 *May it be done to me according to your word.*

Weariness
Psalm 62 *How long will you set yourself against a man?*

Desire to Pray
Luke 11:1–13 *Lord, teach us to pray.*

Praise God
Psalm 96 *Let the heavens be glad.*

Thankfulness
Psalm 92 *You make me jubilant, Lord.*

Close to the Lord
John 15:15–17 *I have called you friends.*

A Guide for the Scrupulous

Fear
Isaiah 44:1–5 — *Do not fear.*

Confusion
Psalm 25 — *Make known to me your ways.*

Hope
Romans 8:28–39 — *Who can be against us?*

A Call to Serve
Acts 22:3–16 — *What shall I do?*

Waiting
Psalm 40 — *Surely, I wait for the Lord.*

Patience
James 5:7–11 — *You too must be patient.*

Memory
Psalm 136 — *The Lord remembered us.*

Healing
1 Corinthians 12:4–11 — *To another gifts of healing by the one Spirit.*

Thirst for God
Psalm 42 — *My soul thirsts for God.*

PART 3: HELPFUL PRAYERS

An Eight-Day Retreat Based on Christian Scripture

The following eight-day retreat introduces some important themes for reflection and prayer that are useful for meditation. The themes build on each other and move you toward an awareness and appreciation of the activity of God at work within yourself.

The suggested readings from Scripture are intended to help focus your attention. It is not necessary or required to complete all the suggested readings for each day. It is helpful to make appropriate notes for each day of the retreat to discuss with the retreat director or with a spiritual director at a future time. These notes may include, but are not limited to, thoughts and emotions you experience while reflecting during times of prayer and meditation.

First Day of Retreat:

God has created me and called me into life.

Suggested Scripture: Psalm 139:1–8; Psalm 8; Jeremiah 18:1–10

Second Day of Retreat:

I am loved by God.

Suggested Scripture: 1 John 4:7–19; Psalm 23; Romans 8:26–34; Romans 5:1–11

Third Day of Retreat:

God desires to be in relationship with me.

Suggested Scripture: Isaiah 43:1–4; Isaiah 49:13–16; John 14:16–28

Fourth Day of Retreat:

All that I have has been given to me by God.

Suggested Scripture: James 1:16–19; 2 Corinthians 4:5–18; John 15:1–8

Fifth Day of Retreat:

God will forgive my transgressions and sins.

Suggested Scripture: Psalm 103; Luke 18:9–14; Romans 8:28–39

PART 3: HELPFUL PRAYERS

Sixth Day of Retreat:

God calls me to live in freedom.

Suggested Scripture: Psalm 42; Hebrews 11:8–19; Philippians 3:7–16

Seventh Day of Retreat:

I am called by God to build the kingdom of God.

Suggested Scripture: John 3:22–30; Luke 1:26–38; 2 Corinthians 12:1–10

Eighth Day of Retreat:

I desire to follow Jesus.

Suggested Scripture: Matthew 8:18–27; 1 Corinthians 1:17–31; Matthew 15

Praying with Ten Companions and Mentors

Prophets and religious teachers are like signs on the road to guide spiritual travelers who become lost in the desert. But those who have attained union with God need nothing but their inner eye and the divine lamp of faith; they need no signs or even a road to travel along. Such people then become signs for others.

RUMI, MASNAVI BOOK II, 3312–14

Each of the companions and mentors that follow are helpful guides for prayer. All are well tested and experienced guides for the spiritual life. For each mystic, there is a particular experience of grace that might be expected as a result of praying with him or her, which is identified in the "Experience of Grace" section. I include these men and women of faith because each one speaks to a particular need or desire that scrupulous people routinely encounter on their spiritual journey. When you are particularly drawn to an experience of grace, it may be beneficial to devote some time and effort to praying with that mystic.

PART 3: HELPFUL PRAYERS

It is not necessary to master the mystic's methodology or mimic his or her experience. It is more than enough to trust the experience itself, believing that the manner in which your experience of grace manifests itself is what is essential and necessary for you. If you discover something useful or develop a perspective that helps you on your spiritual journey, then the mystic has indeed "mentored" you.

Saint Alphonsus Liguori, CSsR

Experience of Grace: Learning that love is the true motivation.

Introduction: Saint Alphonsus Maria Liguori was born on September 27, 1696, in Marianella, Italy, and died on August 1, 1787, in Pagani, Italy. He was canonized in 1839, and his feast day is August 1. A doctor of the Church, St. Alphonsus was one of the chief eighteenth-century moral theologians. In addition to his scholarly expertise and pastoral insight, he is also fondly remembered as the founder of the Redemptorists, a congregation of men dedicated to preaching and bringing witness to the charism of "With Him There Is Plentiful Redemption for All." Saint Alphonsus was dedicated to a tireless work ethic, and the fruits of his work are abundant. He wrote 111 books, including *The Glories of Mary*, one of the most widely used manuals of devotion to the Virgin Mary. By the middle of the twentieth century, his works had gone through several thousand editions and been translated into sixty languages. Saint Alphonsus also painted and wrote music. His song "Gesu Bambino" is the Italian equivalent of our "Silent Night."

PART 3: HELPFUL PRAYERS

In His Own Words

For God, heaven is the human heart. Does God love you? Love him. His delights are to be with you; let yours be to be with him, to pass all your lifetime with him in the delight of whose company you hope to spend a blissful eternity. Accustom yourself to speaking with him alone, familiarly, with confidence and love, as to the dearest friend you have and who loves you best.

THE WAY OF SALVATION AND OF PERFECTION

By praying, our salvation is made secure and very easy. It is not necessary in order to save our souls to go among the heathen and give up our life. It is not necessary to retire into the desert and eat nothing but herbs. What does it cost to say, "My God, help me! Lord, assist me! Have mercy on me!" Is there anything more easy than this? And this little will suffice to save us if we will be diligent in doing it.

PRAYER: THE GREAT MEANS OF SALVATION
AND OF PERFECTION

God wishes all to be saints, and each according to their state of life: the religious as religious, the secular as secular, the priest as priest, the married as married, the businessperson as businessperson, the soldier as soldier, and so of every other state of life.
>> The Practice of the Love of Jesus Christ

God is our only lover who loves us without self-interest and merely because of his goodness. Because he loves us, he wants us to love him with all our hearts.
>> Attaining Salvation: Devout Reflections and Meditations

We must not concentrate so much on what Christ has done for us and suffered for us as on the love with which he did it all.
>> Selva

PART 3: HELPFUL PRAYERS

Prayer Starters / Focus

Saint Alphonsus urges us to pay particular attention to the "mysteries of redemption" in our prayer. For him, this refers to the "crib, cross, and Blessed Sacrament." This is shorthand to help us remember the mysteries of redemption.

Prayer is, first and foremost, the action of God's grace in human nature rather than a purely human activity. Prayer opens us to the will of God, through which we become partners with Jesus in the work of redemption. A petition is not about informing God of our needs or changing God's will; it is about God changing us. It opens up a communion of love with those for whom we pray, and it challenges us to respond to them in love as God as responded to us.

Closing Prayer

My God, I adore you and love you with all my heart. I thank you for all the gifts you have given me, and especially for having preserved me this night. I offer you whatever I may do or suffer this day, in union with the actions and sufferings of Jesus and Mary. I beg you to grant me perseverance for the love of Jesus Christ. I resolve to conform myself to your holy will, and particularly in those things that are contrary to my inclinations. Jesus, keep your hand over me in blessing this day. Amen.

PART 3: HELPFUL PRAYERS

Saint Gerard Majella, CSsR

Experience of Grace: Experience of an intense and loving community that can support us in our individual struggles.

Introduction: Saint Gerard Majella was born on April 6, 1726, in Muro, Italy, and died on October 16, 1755. From his youth, his only ambition was to be like Jesus Christ in his sufferings and humiliations. His father died while St. Gerard was a child, so his pious mother was obliged to apprentice him to a tailor. His reverence for the priesthood and his love of suffering led him to take service in the house of a bishop who was hard to please. When the bishop died, St. Gerard returned to his trade, dividing his earnings between his mother, the poor, and offerings for the souls in purgatory.

Saint Gerard eventually entered the Redemptorist Congregation in 1749. In addition to the usual vows, he added one by which he bound himself to do always that which seemed to him more perfect. Although weak in body, St. Gerard did the work of three, and his great charity earned for him the title of Father of the Poor. As a Redemptorist, he converted many souls while on missions. It is said he predicted the day and hour of his death. A wonderworker during his life, St. Gerard has continued to be the same since his death.

In His Own Words

Who will be able to give us peace except God? When has the world filled the human heart, whether of a princess, a queen, or an empress? This has never yet been heard or read in any book. We only know that the world always sows thorns and tribulations in their hearts, the richer, the more honored and esteemed they were, with a life completely full of satisfactions, they suffered just as much inside.

Consider, I beg you, the brevity of the world and the lastingness of eternity. Think that everything comes to an end. Everything is finished for those who live in the world; it is as if they had never been there. As a result, what good does it do to lean on what cannot sustain us? So, all these things that do not carry us to God are vanity, and they can be of no use to us for eternity. How poor is the person who trusts in the world and not in God.

PART 3: HELPFUL PRAYERS

Prayer Starters / Focus

Saint Gerard demonstrated, by word and example, how to live always united to the Most Holy Redeemer, challenging us to hold dear in our hearts and in our actions those who are most in need. We try to remain sensitive to the harshness and the difficulties that the poor face daily.

Saint Gerard's way of praying was to see God present in all things, people, and events. "If God took this mask away from our eyes, we would see paradise everywhere. Beneath these stones, beneath these rocks, too, is God."

Saint Gerard desired, above all else, to conform his will to the will of God; it was his permanent aspiration, even on his deathbed. He told his confessor, "I imagine that this bed is the will of God, and I am nailed to this bed as if I were nailed to the will of God. Even more, I imagine that the will of God and I have become one and the same thing." Posted on the door of his room was a written sign: "Here the will of God is being done, as God wishes and for as long as God wishes."

Closing Prayer

If I am lost, I lose God. And what is left for me to lose once I have lost God? Lord, make the faith in the most Blessed Sacrament especially alive in me.

I choose the Holy Spirit as my only consoler and protector in all things. Let the Spirit be my advocate and conqueror in all my causes.

And so I trust and hope in God alone, since in his hands I have placed my whole life so that he may do with it what he wishes. I am, then, alive, but without life, because my life is God. I trust in God alone, and only for him do I hope for help in fulfilling truthfully what I pray for today. Love like Jesus and Mary!

Amen.

Saint Thérèse of Lisieux

Experience of Grace: Learning to pray the way you can, instead of praying in a manner that is not helpful for you.

Introduction: Saint Thérèse of the Child Jesus and the Holy Face, better known as the "Little Flower," was born on January 2, 1873, in Alençon, France, and died on September 30, 1897. A young woman, Thérèse and her "little way" have made her one of the most beloved saints. A Carmelite nun who led a cloistered life from the age of fifteen, her short life was filled with the music of knowing she was loved by God, even as she experienced intense moments of doubt and feelings of abandonment by God. Through it all, she prevailed and, at the moment of death, pronounced, "My God, I love you." Saint Thérèse wrote an autobiography and was declared a doctor of the Church in 1997.

In Her Own Words

What an extraordinary thing it is, the efficiency of prayer! Like a queen, it has access at all times to the Royal Presence and can get whatever it asks for. And it is a mistake to imagine that your prayer won't be answered unless you've something out of a book, some splendid formula of words, specially devised to meet this emergency. If that were true, I'm afraid I should be in a terribly bad position. You see, I recite the Divine Office, with a great sense of unworthiness, but apart from that I can't face the strain of hunting about in books for these splendid prayers—it makes my head spin. There are such a lot of them, each more splendid than the last; how am I to recite them all or to choose between them? I just do what children have to do before they've learnt to read; I tell God what I want quite simply, without any splendid turns of phrase, and somehow he always manages to understand me. For me, prayer means launching out of the heart toward God; it means lifting up one's eyes, quite simply, to heaven, a cry of grateful love, from the crest of joy or the trough of despair; it's a vast, supernatural force which opens out my heart and binds me close to Jesus.

AUTOBIOGRAPHY OF ST. THÉRÈSE OF LISIEUX

PART 3: HELPFUL PRAYERS

Prayer Starters / Focus

Saint Thérèse showed us how to live as children of God and challenged us to believe that holiness is for everyone, not just a chosen few. She taught us that holiness does not consist of extraordinary religious experiences but in cooperating with God in the ordinary happenings of everyday life; in the process, gently turning us away from an unhealthy obsession with satisfying God's demanding justice by inviting us to surrender our lives to God's merciful love for us.

Saint Thérèse's way of praying grew intuitively from her great desire to love God. She knew what lovers know: the desire to love is love, and the desire to be totally available to God is prayer. Her desire to pray led her instinctively, even if it was not the way she or others expected.

Saint Thérèse once pictured a person in prayer as a little child instinctively seeking the nourishment of his or her mother. Let your breathing be the center of your attention for a moment. Let your breathing remind you of God's nourishment and care. Be aware of the air filling your lungs and giving you life. As you breathe, let yourself be aware of God, ever present and loving. Rest in God.

Closing Prayer

O my God! I offer thee all my actions of this day for the intentions and for the glory of the Sacred Heart of Jesus. I desire to sanctify every beat of my heart, my every thought, my simplest works, by uniting them to Its infinite merits, and I wish to make reparation for my sins by casting them into the furnace of Its merciful love.

O my God! I ask of thee for myself and for those whom I hold dear, the grace to fulfill perfectly thy holy will, to accept for love of thee the joys and sorrows of this passing life, so that we may one day be united together in heaven for all eternity. Amen.

PART 3: HELPFUL PRAYERS

Saint Catherine of Siena

Experience of Grace: Experience the "inner cell" of the knowledge of God.

Introduction: Saint Catherine of Siena was born in Italy on March 25, 1347, and died on April 29, 1380. She was the youngest of twenty-five children. At a very young age, St. Catherine experienced her first vision of God and, as a result, dedicated her life to solitary prayer and fasting. At the same time, she also actively served in homes and hospitals as a nurse. Although unable to write, St. Catherine dictated her teachings and reflections on prayer, obedience, necessary discipline, and other related spiritual topics to friends and members of her family. She had a profound influence on politics and the life of the Church, convincing the pope to return to Rome, and was declared a doctor of the Church in 1970.

In Her Own Words

If we were to ask the merciful Father how to discover his will, this is how he would answer us: "Dearest children, if you wish to discover and experience the effects of my will, dwell within the cell of your soul." This cell is the well in which there is earth as well as water. In the earth, we can recognize our own poverty: we see that we are not. For we are not. We see that our being is from God. Oh ineffable, blazing Love! I see next that as we discover the earth (our poverty), we get to the living water, the very core of the knowledge of his true and gentle will which desires nothing else but that we be made whole. So let us enter into the depths of that well; for if we dwell there, we will necessarily come to know both ourselves and God's goodness. In recognizing that we are nothing, we humble ourselves. And in humbling ourselves, we enter that flaming, consumed Heart, opened up like a window without shutters, never to be closed. As we focus there the eye of the free will God has given us, we see and know that his will has become nothing other than our sanctification.

Letter to Br. Tommaso dalla Fonte

PART 3: HELPFUL PRAYERS

Prayer Starters / Focus

"God talks and we listen. We then talk to God and then God listens."

"You made four petitions of me with anxious desire, or rather I caused you to make them in order to increase the fire of my love in your soul: to know you through the light of faith, to show mercy to the world, to pray for the mystical body of the Church, and, finally, knowing you as Creator, Protector, and Word."

THE DIALOGUE OF ST. CATHERINE OF SIENA

Closing Prayer

Love, sweet love! Open, open up our memory for us, so that we may receive, hold fast, and understand God's great goodness! For as we understand, so we love, and when we love, we find ourselves united with the transformed in love. Amen.

THE LETTERS OF ST. CATHERINE OF SIENA

Saint Hildegard of Bingen

Experience of Grace: Changing our perspective and seeing that the entire world has been embraced by the Creator's kiss.

Introduction: Saint Hildegard of Bingen was born in Germany in 1098 and died on September 17, 1179. She has been called "one of the most important figures in the history of the Middle Ages" and "the greatest woman of her time." When St. Hildegard was eight years old, she went to a Benedictine monastery to be educated; when she turned eighteen, she became a nun. Twenty years later, she became head of the female community at the monastery. Within the next four years, she had a series of visions and devoted ten years to writing them down, including drawn pictures and comments on their interpretation and significance. Saint Hildegard also traveled throughout southern Germany, Switzerland, and Paris to preach. Her surviving works include more than a hundred letters to emperors, popes, bishops, nuns, and nobility. Saint Hildegard was also a renowned composer and highly knowledgeable about medicinal practices; she was declared a doctor of the Church in 2012.

PART 3: HELPFUL PRAYERS

In Her Own Words

God is the foundation for everything. This God undertakes, God gives. Such that nothing that is necessary for life is lacking. Now humankind always needs a body that honors and praises God. This body is supported in every way through the earth. Thus, the earth glorifies the power of God. As the Creator loves his creation, so creation loves the Creator. Creation, of course, was fashioned to be adorned, to be showered, to be gifted with the love of the Creator. The entire world has been embraced by this kiss. God has gifted creation with everything that is necessary. Limitless love, from the depths to the stars: flooding all, loving all. It is the royal kiss of peace.

Prayer Starters / Focus

Saint Hildegard would have us understand that the love between Creator and creature can be compared to the love of husband and wife in vowed fidelity. Creation speaks to the Creator as a lover and dares to participate in its own co-creation. The implications are clear—justice for all humankind and compassion for the earth. "I compare the great love of Creator and creation to the same love and fidelity with which God binds woman and man together. This is so that together they might be creatively fruitful so that the entire world might be embraced by this kiss."

Saint Hildegard understands that the Word is living, being, spirit, all verdant greening, all creativity. The Word manifests itself in every creature. Creation is a profound and divine blessing, and in the wonderful harmony and balance of all things in creation, we learn the lesson of sufficiency: "God has arranged all things in the world in consideration of everything else."

Saint Hildegard understands the earth as the mother of all that is natural, mother of all that is human. Humankind itself is an "earth" that contains all moistness, all verdancy, all germinating power. From the earth came the substance of the Incarnation of God's Son. Saint Hildegard embraced the concepts of earthiness and sexuality, which stands in opposition to the traditional Augustinian viewpoint of creation, which declares that "the soul makes war with the body."

PART 3: HELPFUL PRAYERS

Closing Prayer

God has created me. God is my Lord, having dominion over me. God is also my strength, for I can wish to do nothing good without God. Through God, I have living Spirit. Through God, I have life and movement. Through God, I learn, I find my path. If I call in truth, this God and Lord directs my steps, setting my feet to the rhythm of his precepts. I run like a deer that seeks its spring. I have my home on high; I meet every creature of the world with grace. I am the delight and illumination of the love of God, the form of all seeking for him. All that God wills, I will. Now I seek no more, desire no more, wish no more but what is holy. Incarnating, you have redeemed me; dying, you have awakened me. Amen.

Meister Eckhart

Experience of Grace: Finding the beautiful, joyful, and familiar path through detachment.

Introduction: Meister Eckhart, born Johannes Eckhart in 1260 in Germany, died in 1327 in Avignon, France. He was a Dominican theologian and writer who was the greatest German speculative mystic. In the transcripts of his sermons, he charted the course of union between the individual soul and God.

Meister Eckhart entered the Dominican Order when he was fifteen and studied in Cologne. In his mid-thirties, he was nominated Vicar (the main Dominican official) of Thuringia and taught theology in Paris, where he received his master's degree and became known as Meister Eckhart.

Meister Eckhart wrote four treatises and the *Talks of Instruction*, a work about self-denial, the nobility of will and intellect, and obedience to God. He became provincial of the Dominicans in Saxony and Vicar of Bohemia. His main role was preaching to the contemplative nuns established throughout the Rhine Valley.

PART 3: HELPFUL PRAYERS

In His Own Words

If we perform our works to go to heaven, we are simply on the wrong track. And until we learn to work without any why or wherefore, we have not learned to work, or to live, or why. Some people, I swear, want to love God in the same way as they love a cow. They love it for its milk and cheese and the profit they will derive from it. Those who love God for the sake of outward riches or for the sake of inward consolation operate on the same principle. They are not loving God correctly; they are merely loving their own advantage.

One Hail Mary uttered sincerely is more potent and better than a thousand uttered mechanically, for the heart is not made pure by prayer, but rather prayer is made pure by the pure heart.

Prayer Starters / Focus

The teachings of Meister Eckhart describe four stages of the union between the soul and God:

1. Dissimilarity
2. Similarity
3. Identity
4. Breakthrough

At the outset, God is all, the creature is nothing; at the ultimate stage, "The soul is above God." The driving power of this process is detachment. Meister Eckhart was part of the Creation-centered spiritual tradition. While the Fall-Redemption tradition begins with humanity's sinfulness, the Creation-centered tradition begins with humanity's potential to act divinely, both by way of compassion and of beauty-making and sharing. This tradition believes that life itself—living and dying, growing and sinning—is the creative energy of God in motion. Meister Eckhart learned to trust life and his own life experiences, teaching others to do this as well. As important as knowledge is for our lives, the spiritual way begins with the heart. To be spiritual is to be awake and alive. For Meister Eckhart, creation itself was the primary sacrament.

PART 3: HELPFUL PRAYERS

Closing Prayer

When one has learned to let go and let be, then one is disposed, and he or she is always in the right place, whether in society or in solitude. But if one has a wrong attitude, one is always in the wrong place, whether in society or not. No one who is rightly disposed has God with one in actual fact in all places, just as much in the street and in the midst of many people and in church, or the desert, or a monastic cell. All paths lead to God, for God is on them all evenly for the person who knows with transformed knowledge. What is best is to take God and enjoy God in any manner, in anything, and not to have to exercise and hunt around for your own special way. All my life this has been my joy! Amen.

Saint Teresa of Calcutta

Experience of Grace: Growing in a daily awareness of the living presence of the will of God.

Introduction: Saint Teresa, better known as Mother Teresa, was born on August 26, 1910, in Macedonia and died on September 5, 1997, in India. At the age of eighteen, she joined the Sisters of Loreto in Ireland and chose the name of Sister Teresa, in memory of St. Thérèse of Lisieux. In 1929, she arrived in Calcutta, India, to teach at a school for girls. While in Calcutta, she was moved by the presence of the sick and dying on the city's streets.

Mother Teresa established her religious community, the Missionaries of Charity, where they gathered dying Indians off the streets of Calcutta and brought them to a home to care for them. Thousands of people died in an environment of kindness and love. Mother Teresa was canonized in 2016, and her congregation continues its mission around the world today.

PART 3: HELPFUL PRAYERS

In Her Own Words

I see God in every human being. When I wash the leper's wounds, I feel I am nursing the Lord himself. Is it not a beautiful experience?

The poor give us much more than we give them. They're such strong people, living day to day with no food. And they never curse, never complain. We don't have to give them pity or sympathy. We have so much to learn from them.

There is a terrible hunger for love. We all experience that in our lives—the pain, the loneliness. We must have the courage to recognize it. The poor you may have right in your own family. Find them. Love them. Put your love for them in living action. For in loving them, you are loving God himself.

It is not how much we do but how much love we put in the doing. It is not how much we give but how much love we put in the giving.

To God there is nothing small. The moment we have given it to God, it becomes infinite.

You have to be holy in your position as you are, and I have to be holy in the position that God has put me. So, it is nothing extraordinary to be holy. Holiness is not the luxury of the few. Holiness is a simple duty for you and for me. We have been created for that.

Prayer Starters / Focus

There are some people who, in order not to pray, use as an excuse the fact that life is so hectic that it prevents them from praying. This cannot be. Prayer does not demand that we interrupt our work but that we continue working as if it were a prayer. It is not necessary to always be meditating, nor to consciously experience the sensation that we are talking to God, no matter how nice this would be. What matters is being with him, living in him, in his will. To love with a pure heart, to love everybody, especially to love the poor, is a twenty-four-hour prayer.

1. The first requirement for prayer is silence. People of prayer are people of silence.
2. My secret is a very simple one. I pray. To pray to Christ is to love him.
3. Prayer is not asking. Prayer is putting oneself in the hands of God, at his disposition and listening to his voice in the depths of our hearts.

PART 3: HELPFUL PRAYERS

4. Every day at Communion time, I communicate two of my feelings to Jesus. One is gratefulness, because he has helped me to persevere until today. The other is a request: "Teach me to pray."

Closing Prayer

Dear Jesus, help me to spread thy fragrance everywhere I go. Flood my soul with thy spirit and love. Penetrate and possess my whole being so utterly that all my life may only be a radiance of thine. Shine through me and be so in me that every soul I encounter may feel thy presence in my soul. Let them look up and see no longer me but only Jesus. Stay with me, and then I shall begin to shine as you shine, so to shine as to be a light to others. Amen.

Saint Teresa of Ávila

Experience of Grace: Praying in darkness and in light.

Introduction: Saint Teresa was born into the Spanish nobility on March 28, 1515, and died on October 4, 1582. Crippled by disease in her youth, she was cured after praying to St. Joseph. She grew up reading about the saints and playing "hermit." Saint Teresa entered a Carmelite house at seventeen. Soon after taking her vows, she became gravely ill and never fully recovered her health. She began receiving visions and was examined by Dominicans and Jesuits, who pronounced the visions to be holy and true. Saint Teresa founded a reformed Carmelite order, the Discalced Carmelites, with St. John of Ávila, and built many convents. She is considered one of the greatest mystical writers and was proclaimed a doctor of the Church in 1970.

In Her Own Words

Whoever has not begun the practice of prayer, I beg for the love of the Lord not to go without so great a good. There is nothing here to fear; there is only something to desire. Even if there be no great progress or much effort in reaching such perfection as to deserve the favor and mercies God bestows on the more generous, at least a person will come to understand the road leading to heaven. And if one perseveres, I trust then in the mercy of God, who never fails to repay anyone who has taken him for a friend. For mental prayer in my opinion is nothing else than an intimate sharing between friends; it means taking time frequently to be alone with him who we know loves us.

THE LIFE OF ST. TERESA OF JESUS:
THE AUTOBIOGRAPHY OF TERESA OF ÁVILA

Prayer Starters / Focus

Prayer is the heart of St. Teresa of Ávila's life and teaching, her "way of perfection." For her, prayer was the supreme meaning and value of human existence, because it is the inner life that animates the exterior—the journey within that is the journey into reality. Prayer is life before it is an exercise, a dimension of being before it is an experience. Prayer means to be in touch with the center of one's life, who is the "Divine Majesty."

The kernel of St. Teresa's mystical thought throughout her writings is the ascent of the soul in four stages:

1. The first, "heart's devotion," is that of devout

contemplation or concentration, the withdrawal of the soul from without and especially the devout observance of the passion of Christ and penitence.

2. The second is "devotion of peace," in which at least the human will is lost in that of God by virtue of a charismatic, supernatural state given of God, while the other faculties, such as memory, reason, and imagination, are not yet secure from worldly distraction.

3. The third, "devotion of union," is not only supernatural but also an essentially ecstatic state. Here, there is also an absorption of the reason in God, and only the memory and imagination are left to ramble. This state is characterized by a blissful peace, a sweet slumber of at least the higher soul faculties, and a conscious rapture in the love of God.

4. The fourth is "devotion of ecstasy or rapture," a passive state in which the consciousness of being in the body disappears. (See 2 Corinthians 12:2–3.) Sensory activity ceases; memory and

imagination are also absorbed in God. Body and spirit are in the throes of a sweet, happy pain, alternating between a fearful fiery glow, a complete impotence, and unconsciousness.

Closing Prayer

Let nothing trouble you,
Let nothing scare you,
All is passing,

God alone is unchanging.

Patience,
God overcomes all.

Who possesses God wants for nothing.

God alone is enough.

Amen.

Thomas Merton, OCSO

Experience of Grace: Discovering the God whom you seek.

Introduction: Thomas Merton, a Trappist monk, was born on January 15, 1915, in France and died on December 10, 1968, in Thailand. Merton won fame for his autobiography, *The Seven Storey Mountain,* which describes Merton's troubled youth and the experiences that led him to become a Catholic in 1938. In 1949, Merton was ordained a Catholic priest and in 1965, he retired to a hermitage. Merton wrote more than forty books, many of which record his struggle for greater personal integrity. He also wrote widely on Eastern religions. He is known as one of the most popular spiritual writers of his time.

PART 3: HELPFUL PRAYERS

In His Own Words

Strictly speaking, I have a very simple way of praying. It is centered entirely on attention to the presence of God and to his will and his love. That is to say, it is centered on faith, by which alone we can know the presence of God. One might say this gives my meditation the character described by the Prophet as "being before God as if you saw him." Yet, it does not mean imagining anything or conceiving a precise image of God, for, to my mind, this would be a kind of idolatry. On the contrary, it is a matter of adoring him as invisible and infinitely beyond our comprehension.... There is in my heart this great thirst to recognize totally the nothingness of all that is not God. My prayer is then a kind of praise rising up out of the center of nothing and silence.

CENTERED ON FAITH, LETTER TO ABDUL AZIZ

Prayer Starters / Focus

At the core of Thomas Merton's spiritual writings is the search for the "true self" and our need for relationship with God, other people, and all of creation. He finds that when we are apart from God, we experience alienation and desolation. Merton concludes that we must discover God as the center of our being to which all things tend and to whom all of our activity must be directed.

In your prayer, you might consider any of the following: What have you learned in life, both the good and the difficult? Embrace and accept who you are as a person. Identify your deepest desires, wishes, hopes, and dreams. Pray for the people in your life who have loved you, challenged you, and mentored you. Move toward an appreciation of the mystery and the wonder of your life.

Either you look at the universe as a very poor creation out of which no one can make anything, or you look at your own life and your own part in the universe as infinitely rich, full of inexhaustible interest, opening out into the infinite further possibilities for study and contemplation and praise. Beyond all and in all is God.

PART 3: HELPFUL PRAYERS

Closing Prayer

My Lord God, I have no idea where I am going. I do not see the road ahead of me. I cannot know for certain where it will end. Nor do I really know myself, and the fact that I think I am following your will does not mean that I am actually doing so. But I believe that the desire to please you does in fact please you. And I hope I have that desire in all that I am doing. I hope that I will never do anything apart from that desire. And I know that if I do this, you will lead me by the right road, though I may know nothing about it. Therefore, I will trust you always, though I may seem to be lost and in the shadow of death. I will not fear, for you are ever with me, and you will never leave me to face my perils alone. Amen.

C.S. Lewis

Experience of Grace: Discovering what you yearn for.

Introduction: Clive Staples Lewis was born on November 29, 1898, in England and died on November 22, 1963. He was a British author and wrote more than thirty books, including children's stories, science fiction, and religious works. Most of his writings teach moral lessons. After years of religious doubt, he converted to Christianity in the 1930s and became a leading defender of Christianity.

Lewis taught medieval literature at Oxford University and Cambridge University. His most popular religious work, *The Screwtape Letters,* is a witty satire in which an old devil advises a young devil. His other books on religion are written in the same style and have been inspirational for many Christian denominations. C.S. Lewis is also famous for the children's series *The Chronicles of Narnia*, which combines fantasy with moral principles.

PART 3: HELPFUL PRAYERS

In His Own Words

The settled happiness and security which we all desire, God withholds from us by the very nature of the world, but joy, pleasure, and merriment he has scattered broadcast. We are never safe, but we have plenty of fun, and some ecstasy. It is not hard to see why. The security we crave would teach us to rest our hearts in this world and oppose an obstacle to our return to God; a few moments of happy love, a landscape, a symphony, a merry meeting with our friends, a bath or a football match, have no such tendency. Our Father refreshes us on the journey with some pleasant inns but will not encourage us to mistake them for home.

The Problem of Pain

Prayer Starters / Focus

Prayer is either a sheer illusion or a personal contact between embryonic, incomplete persons (ourselves) and the utterly concrete Person. Prayer in the sense of petition, asking for things, is a small part of it; confession and penitence are its threshold, adoration its sanctuary, the presence and vision and enjoyment of God its bread and wine. In it, God shows himself to us. That he answers prayers is a corollary—not necessarily the most important one—from that revelation. What he does is learned from what he is.

The World's Last Night: And Other Essays

A man can no more diminish God's glory by refusing to worship him than a lunatic can put out the sun by scribbling the word "darkness" on the walls of his cell.

The Problem of Pain

Aim at heaven and you will get earth thrown in. Aim at earth and you get neither.

The Joyful Christian

PART 3: HELPFUL PRAYERS

God cannot give us a happiness and peace apart from himself because it is not there. There is no such thing.
                                        Mere Christianity

I gave in and admitted that God was God.
                Surprised by Joy: The Shape of My Early Life

It may be hard for an egg to turn into a bird; it would be a jolly sight harder for it to learn to fly while remaining an egg. We are like eggs at present. And you cannot go on indefinitely being just an ordinary, decent egg. We must be hatched or go bad.
                                        Mere Christianity

Miracles are a retelling in small letters of the very same story which is written across the whole world in letters too large for some of us to see.

There are two kinds of people: those who say to God, "Thy will be done," and those to whom God says, "All right, then, have it your way."
                                        The Great Divorce

Closing Prayer

[God], we acknowledge that you could, if you so choose to do so, might repair our bodies miraculously without food; or give us food without the aid of farmers, bakers, and butchers; or knowledge without the aid of learned men and women; or convert the heathen without missionaries. Instead, you allow soils and weather and animals and the muscles, minds, and wills of men and women to cooperate in the execution of your will....
Help us Lord, when we pray, to make this act no more than any of all our other acts, or to be separated from you in any way, for we acknowledge that upon you alone we live, move, and have our being this day. Amen.

Notes From the Author

Some of the material in this book originally appeared in *Sacred Refuge: Why and How to Make a Retreat,* by Rev. Thomas M. Santa, CSsR (Ave Maria Press, 2005). This original work is out of print, and all rights have reverted to the author. The material presented here has been significantly reworked, expanded, and edited for the readers of this edition.

Many of the reflections in the "Spiritual Practices" and "Critical Beliefs" sections originally appeared in various editions of *Scrupulous Anonymous* newsletter, produced by Liguori Publications. In each instance, the material has been significantly reworked, expanded, and edited for the readers of this edition. Rev. Thomas M. Santa, CSsR, is the copyright owner. Each previously published newsletter is used by Liguori Publications only for the named volume and number.

The material in "Praying with Ten Companions and Mentors" is the result of an ongoing collaboration between the author, Rev. Ken Sedlak, CSsR, and Rev. Paul Coury, CSsR. In its original format, titled *Praying With the Mystics,* it was used in programs at St. Michael's Parish in Chicago and the Redemptorist Renewal Center in Tucson, and is used in this book with their permission.

The meditations on the holy Eucharist were originally collected in the ascetical works of St. Alphonsus, arranged and translated from the Italian by Rev. Eugene Grimm, CSsR. The meditations appeared in Volume 6 of *The Holy Eucharist*, under the original title "Meditations for the Octave of Corpus Christi." The author has excerpted and prepared these meditations for private prayer and devotion specifically for this book.

In any work of this type, the material acquired, edited, and perfected through years of pastoral work will have the occasional duplication of a resource that may not be sufficiently referenced. Although every attempt has been made to collect the necessary permissions and to provide the required documentation, it is possible that the occasional reference or resource may not be sufficiently documented. If any reader recognizes text in this work that is not properly documented, please bring this oversight to the attention of the author, and the correction will be immediately applied to this work and any future editions.

Bibliography

Scripture quotations are taken from *The New American Bible, Revised Edition* © 2010, 1991, 1986, 1970 Confraternity of Christian Doctrine, Washington, D.C., and are used by permission of the copyright owner. All Rights Reserved. No part of *The New American Bible* may be reproduced in any form without permission in writing from the copyright owner.

Quoted prayers by Thomas Merton, Henry Viscardi, Anselm of Canterbury, and Charles de Foucauld are from *Orientations, Vol. I: A Collection of Helps for Prayer* by John Veltri, SJ (Loyola House, 1979).

Brussat, Frederic and Mary Ann. *Spiritual Literacy, Reading the Sacred in Everyday Life.* New York: Scribner, 1998.

Buxbaum, Yitzhak. *Jewish Spiritual Practices.* Northvale, NJ: Jason Aronson, Inc., 1999.

de Mello, Anthony. *Awareness: Conversations with the Masters.* New York: Doubleday Religion, 1990.

Foster, Nelson, and Jack Shoemaker. *The Roaring Stream: A New Zen Reader.* New York: Ecco Press, 1997.

Harvey, Andrew. *A Walk With Four Spiritual Guides: Krishna, Buddha, Jesus, and Ramakrishna.* Nashville, TN: SkyLight Paths Publishing, 2005.

King, Ursula. *Christian Mystics: Their Lives and Legacies Throughout the Ages.* Mahwah, NJ: HiddenSpring, 2001.

Rolheiser, Ronald. *The Holy Longing: The Search for a Christian Spirituality.* New York: Doubleday, 1999.

Santa, Thomas M. *Understanding Scrupulosity, Third Edition.* Liguori, MO: Liguori Publications, 2015.

———. *Christian Contemplative Living: Six Connecting Points.* Chicago: In Extenso Press, 2014.

Bibliography

Tolle, Eckhart. *Stillness Speaks*. Novato, CA: New World Library, 2003.

Walsh, Roger, MD, PhD. *Essential Spirituality, Exercises from the World's Religions to Cultivate Kindness, Love, Joy, Peace, Vision, Wisdom, and Generosity.* New York: John Wiley & Sons, Inc., 1999.

About the Author

Rev. Thomas M. Santa, CSsR, is the president and publisher of Liguori Publications, his second assignment as the company's leader. Professed as a Redemptorist in 1973, Fr. Santa has engaged in a variety of ministries, including retreat work; serving for many years as the spiritual director and a pastoral counselor for clients who access the ManagingScrupulosity.com website; and writing reflections and answering reader questions for decades in Liguori Publications' *Scrupulous Anonymous* newsletter.

www.ingramcontent.com/pod-product-compliance
Lightning Source LLC
Chambersburg PA
CBHW070640160426
43194CB00009B/1520